The Searcher of Hearts

The Searcher of Hearts

sermon notes on Romans 8 verses 26 - 34
by John Newton

transcribed and edited
by
Marylynn Rouse

Christian Heritage

© Marylynn Rouse
ISBN 1 85792 314 6
Published in 1997
in the Christian Heritage imprint by
Christian Focus Publications,
Geanies House, Fearn, Ross-shire,
IV20 1TW, Great Britain

Cover design by Donna Macleod

Contents

Since all that I meet
Shall work for my good,
The bitter is sweet,
The med'cine is food;
Tho' painful at present,
'Twill cease before long,
And then, oh! how pleasant,
The conqueror's song!

John Newton

PREFACE

This book is part of a series of lectures on Romans 8, previously unpublished, which John Newton preached at the midweek meetings of his church, St. Peter and St. Paul, in Olney. It was for these meetings that he and William Cowper, whom Newton called his *alter idem*, began composing hymns. Amongst these was 'Begone Unbelief', which draws directly from Romans 8 for its last verse, quoted overleaf, being, as Newton says of all his hymns, 'the fruit and expression of my own experience.'[1]

This rich combination of Biblical truth and experience had a profound effect on the lives of many who heard him or read his publications.

Shortly after moving to Olney, Cowper wrote to his aunt, 'The Lord ... has graciously given me my heart's desire.... To be brought under the ministry of so wise and faithful a steward of his holy mysteries is a blessing for which I can never be sufficiently thankful.'[2]

Newton's hymns have been favourites of mine for many years. Coming across these manuscripts has been a tremendous privilege and has been part of a spiritual renewal in my life.

After some months' illness and spiritual dryness I picked up a church magazine. On the back was a verse which spoke strongly to me in a way I hadn't experienced for some years. *'My heart has heard you say, "Come and talk with me, O my people." And my heart responds, "Lord I am coming."'*[3]

As a result I began attending the Baptist Church in Stratford, where the combination of prayerful and scriptural teaching and the warmth and reality of the people's belief began to rekindle my own faith. I found myself waking early in the morning and spending time searching the Scriptures. While reading Jonah, I was struck by a similarity with Newton's experience at sea, which I'd read of in John Pollock's biography, *Amazing Grace*. A phrase in Jonah 2:8 – '*the grace that could be theirs*'[4] – seemed to illustrate the lost and gained experiences of the various characters and to link in with this.

A trip to the Bodleian Library in Oxford revealed several of Newton's books, where I was intrigued to read that Newton, in his unconverted and blasphemous state, had been called a Jonah by the ship's captain and had been in fear of being thrown overboard to lessen their troubles.

I visited Newton's church in Olney to see where he had preached during those sixteen years of his ministry. There I discovered a pamphlet advertising the Cowper and Newton Museum where some of his original manuscripts were available to study.[5] Amongst these were two pocket notebooks in Newton's handwriting, labelled Vol 4 and Vol 5, containing Lectures 31 to 58 on Romans 8:26-34.

Mrs Elizabeth Knight, Custodian of the Museum, kindly gave me access to the notebooks and other research material. The lectures contained such useful instruction that I was keen to see them made more widely available. I am very grateful to William MacKenzie and Christian Focus for the opportunity to publish them.

The Searcher of Hearts is a recurring phrase in the lectures on verse 27. It seems so fitting a description from one who knew both the hidden depths of his own heart and the gracious assistance of the Searcher. Indeed Newton's close friend, Richard Cecil, said of his writings: 'They are the language of the heart: they show a deep experience of its religious feelings; a continual anxiety to sympathize with man in his wants, and to direct him to his only resources.... His grand point, in a few words, as he used to express it, was, "to break a hard heart and to heal a broken heart".'[6]

In transcribing Newton's handwriting I have modernised the spelling and punctuation to make it more easily readable, but there are essentially no changes to the text. Specific details of editing can be found in the Appendix. I strongly recommend looking up the scripture references quoted in the lectures as they occur. It is interesting also to note Newton's use of local scenery, the market in Olney, and local trades such as watchmaking for his illustrations.

My thanks to Tony Baker for first inspiring an appreciation of Newton in the '70s while vicar of Redlands Parish Church, Bristol, and for his encouragement in pursuing this project. Thanks also to Redlanders Betty Waters and Margaret Wilkins for their help and to friends at Stratford Baptist Church for their encouragement and support, especially my pastor and his wife, Albert and Pam Yorke. I am grateful to Alison Balaam, Classics lecturer at Warwick University, for comparing the Greek references with the Textus Receptus.

There were probably about seventy lectures in all on Romans 8. Newton wrote to Capt. Alexander Clunie[7] in January 1766, saying that he had just started on verse 36 and expected to spend three or four lectures on that. At the beginning of April he mentioned that he had just finished the Romans 8 lectures and 'by way of epilogue to them' preached from John 13:17.

In a letter to the Revd. Mr. Symonds of Bedford[8], Newton says: 'I intend to send you herewith the notes of my lectures on Romans 8 which I beg you to take care and return to me as soon as convenient; they are in 6 books.' Over the years Newton's manuscripts have become widely dispersed. Should anyone know the whereabouts of the other four notebooks we would be very glad to know!

Marylynn Rouse
Stratford-on-Avon 1997

References

1. Newton's preface to Olney Hymns, 1779, republished 1979 for the Cowper and Newton Museum
2. William Cowper to his aunt Mrs Madan, Sept. 26, 1767
3. Psalm 27.8 (Living Bible)
4. New International Version
5. These are now kept in the County Archives in Aylesbury Record Office
6. Richard Cecil, *Memoirs of the Rev. John Newton.*
7. John Newton, *The Christian Correspondent*, 1790.
8. John Newton to the Revd. Mr. Symonds, 23 August, 1771. Joshua Symonds was pastor of Bunyan Meeting. He and John Ryland stayed at the vicarage with Newton while all three of them attended the Northamptonshire Baptist Association Meetings in Olney. 'Poor thing,' wrote Newton to his wife, 'he never seems to have enough of my company, such as it is.'

CHAPTER ONE

verse 26 (1)

Likewise the Spirit also helpeth our infirmities: for we know not what we should pray for as we ought: but the Spirit itself maketh intercession for us with groanings which cannot be uttered.

As the afflictions and crosses of the Christian life are manifold, so likewise are the arguments of comfort which God has provided to support us under them. Of these a principal one is the consideration of the end to which they lead – the glory which shall be revealed. If we suffer with him we shall also reign with him. Of the nature, certainty, proofs of this blessed hope the Apostle has been treating in the preceding verses from verse 17 to the close of verse 25. He now proceeds to a second source of consolation, that respects not the future but the present. We not only hope for a happy issue of all our troubles at last, but even now in the midst of all complaints and distress, we are not alone. We may be cast down but shall not be forsaken. The believer is not only distressed by many enemies and trials from without, but by a sense of many infirmities within. But though we are weak we cannot be overpowered, for the Spirit is promised and vouchsafed to help our infirmities.

Here are several particulars worthy of our notice:

1. The believer's weakness in him: he has *infirmities* – not one but many.

2. One particular and chief infirmity specified: *we know not how to pray as we ought.*

3. The relief under this and all our other infirmities: *the Spirit helpeth*.

4. The manner of this help: *maketh intercession*.

5. The earnestness of this: *with groanings which cannot be uttered*.

1. Infirmities

By infirmities here, I suppose the Apostle does not mean the proper and direct fruits of the sinful principle yet remaining in us, but only the effect of it so far as it keeps all our graces in a weak and languid state. Whatever can be accounted good in us is not only not our own but is mixed and debased by being put into such polluted vessels, as the best wine will taste of any impurity in the cask that contains it. Thus all our graces are in a state of imperfection and weakness and give occasion to manifest our great infirmities. Instance in:

1.1 A spiritual understanding

This all believers have received, whereby they know what once they knew not and which others are still ignorant of. The things of God are not altogether foolishness to them but they live and feed upon them. Yet not without infirmity.

(i) Much darkness in the faculty. So that they can hardly reconcile some truths and perhaps for a season cannot at all receive others.

(ii) Ignorance with respect to the object. What they know after their manner is but little in comparison with what they know not.

(iii) Their notion of judgment, though weak and faint at the best, is still much more considerable than their real experience.

1.2 Faith
A measure of this they have as to its reality, but as to its degree – alas what infirmity. It is:

(i) Weak
Very disproportionate to the appointed grounds: (a) the word of God; (b) their past experience.

(ii) Wavering
If they get a little enlargement at times, they can seldom hold it long, but are prone upon every little change to fall back to their old dullness.

1.3 Love
This is sincere. They love the Lord. He is their heart's desire, their settled choice, but in nothing do their infirmities more distress them than in this. They find:

(i) A proneness to cleave to creatures and to seek some part of their rest in them.

(ii) Too much impatience when their idols are taken away and their cisterns broken. Both these evils proceed from and evidence the weakness of their love.

The infirmities attending their knowledge, faith and love produce proportionable abatements in:

1.4 Obedience
This gracious principle is deeply rooted in their hearts. They delight in the law of God after the inner man. But when they

would do good, evil is present with them. They are subject to mistake.

(i) The rule
The word of God is exceeding broad and their minds are narrow. If they are diligent in one part of duty, they are apt to overlook something equally necessary. If they are careful to avoid one extreme they are apt to verge too near the other.

(ii) The means
Too liable to forget that their whole is in Christ and that of themselves they can do nothing.

(iii) The end
Their professed end is the will and glory of him who has called them and they willingly allow of no other. But through infirmity, such mean and selfish ends at some times fall in with these, as when discovered fill them with shame.

1.5 Prayer

The infirmities they labour under with respect to prayer and their especial need of the Spirit's assistance in this behalf is particularly noticed in my text, but this I proposed to make a separate head, and as it is a point of great importance, I shall defer the consideration to our next opportunity.

At present we may observe from what has been said:

1. What reason the best of us have to say with David: Psalm 130.3, 4. Well may we praise God for an Advocate and High Priest who can *bear* and *bear with* the iniquity of our holy things.

2. What a wonder of grace and power is it that any, even the best of the sons [of] men, should be brought safe to glory. A view of our infirmities, together with the many snares and enemies around us and the power and subtlety of Satan, who knows how to fit us with suitable temptations, may almost make us cry out, who then can be saved? But Jesus is all sufficient. His strength is made perfect in our weakness. May he have all the glory.

3. Let each one put it to themselves. Have you such a sense of your own infirmities? Has your heart gone along with me and said under each particular, so I find it?

If so, take comfort – you are in the right road. To have these gracious dispositions and to feel your own deficiencies under each is a sure mark of a work of grace. And he that has begun will carry it on.

But if not, if the characters of the children of God in the word do not answer to your experience, the plain consequence is that as yet you are not one of them. That is in other words you are still in your sins, a child of wrath and under the curse. And can you go quickly to sleep tonight with this thought? O rather cry to the Lord for mercy, while mercy may be found.

CHAPTER TWO
verse 26 (2)

*Likewise the Spirit also helpeth our infirmities: for we know not
what we should pray for as we ought: but the Spirit itself maketh
intercession for us with groanings which cannot be uttered.*

Besides the infirmities attending our knowledge, faith, love
and obedience, there is an especial mention of one in my text,
respectively prayer. This is the point:

2. We know not how to pray as we ought

If we could pray as we ought we should soon gain ground of
our other infirmities, for effectual fervent prayer availeth much.
Prayer is a main piece of our spiritual armour. Prayer is a chief
part of our spiritual food. With good reason therefore this infirmity is particularly mentioned because it has a main influence upon all the rest. The grace we exercise in prayer is the
measure of all our other graces. The Spirit helps our infirmities in prayer, as the chief means of giving us victory over the
others.

The Apostle does not deny but [that] we may in general
from the word of God know how we ought to pray – we may
know so as to direct others – but then we know not to reduce[1]
our knowledge by experience, to practice the rules after we
have got and actually to pray both for matter and manner as
we ought.

2.1. As to matter,

Our petitions should be:

(i) Limited to those things which are really good for us.
But here we are ignorant. We ask and receive not because
we ask amiss (James 4.3; Mark 10.38).

16

Again we ought to ask all those things which we really need, but alas how short-sighted are we as to our true wants, how many things should we forget.

(ii) Governed by the promises.
So as to expect nothing beyond them and not to rest short of the whole. Surely whatever God has thought proper to promise, is worth our while to ask.

2.2 As to the manner
We ought to pray:

(i) With the deepest sense of our own unworthiness. So Abraham (Gen. 18.27).

(ii) With the most profound reverence of the Divine Majesty.

(iii) With the most perfect submission to his wise and holy will.

(iv) In faith. Or else how can we expect to receive? (James 1.6,7).

(v) With patience and perseverance.

Whoever has any spiritual sense or feeling must be convinced how greatly deficient he is in all these respects. And whatever little measure we have attained to is by the Spirit's help. At best we pray but poorly, but of ourselves we know not at all how to pray as we ought. Blessed be God, the Spirit is promised to make intercession for us or rather in us. Of this hereafter.

Hence see:

1. The guilt and danger of those who are so far from praying as they ought, that they do not pray. The little that is said here plainly implies that prayer is a matter:

1.1 Of duty
And heavy judgments are denounced against those who live without it. Though men may speak well of you the Lord abhors you, and his word condemns you, if you live without prayer.

1.2 Of necessity
This is plain if we have many wants, if God alone can supply them and if he has restrained[2] his assistance to those who seek him with their whole hearts.

2. The mistake of those who account prayer an easy thing. The awakened soul does not find it so. It is the most difficult because the most spiritual service and would be wholly impracticable without the assistance of the Spirit.

3. The proper assistance against our infirmities is the Spirit. Nothing else will do. Forms of prayer in public devotion appear to me in all circumstances lawful, in some expedient, in some perhaps quite necessary and may be very useful to those who are beginning to set up the worship of God in their families, but even these are utterly vain and useless unless the Spirit helps us to understand and feel the meaning of what is thus prepared to our hands. However in the private exercises between God and our own souls – if we have any true knowledge of our case – we should either not need the help of books, or find a variety of desires which no book can help us to express. People do not want forms and books to teach them how to manage their business at market – the reason is because they understand what they are about there and their hearts are set upon it. So it is in spiritual concerns.

4. What an encouragement here is to those who are sincerely desirous to pray acceptably. You find you are not able of yourselves, but you see the Spirit is promised. Make this therefore your first petition. If you can say no more say, Lord teach us to pray. See how graciously the promise runs: Luke 11.13. Make trial and you shall find it was not given in vain.

CHAPTER THREE

verse 26 (3)

Likewise the Spirit also helpeth our infirmities: for we know not what we should pray for as we ought: but the Spirit itself maketh intercession for us with groanings which cannot be uttered.

The consideration of our many infirmities, the weakness of our graces and the unworthiness of our prayers, ought to humble us, to shut our mouths for ever as to boasting and make us willing to give all the glory to the Lord. However we need not, we should not, be cast down, for here is comfort – the Spirit is promised and many who have no sufficiency in themselves can say in the words of the text – the Spirit helpeth our infirmities. This is then:

3. The Spirit helpeth

The word is used (Luke 10.40) which leads to the proper sense and affords occasion for observing:

3.1 That the assistance of the Spirit does not supersede the necessity of diligence on our parts in the use of means. Some greatly mistake this matter, as if the Spirit moved the heart by an external force as we move great logs and stones. The Spirit's influence is vital and inward – as the warmth of the sun powerfully yet gently operates upon the sap of plants and moves them to produce leaves, flowers and fruits in a way agreeable to their own nature, so the Spirit works upon our renewed natures in the use of proper and appointed means. He works in us first to will and then to do of his own good pleasure. The soul is made to see the value and need of this Helper – to plead the promise of his help – to wait in his way and to strive together with him.

3.2 That the Spirit does not remove our infirmities entirely but helps us against them. We must not expect such assistance as shall leave us no more cause of complaint and infirmities – we shall have reason to confess ourselves poor sinners to the end of our lives. Many burthen themselves and will take no comfort because they expect more than God has promised. Strive against infirmity and sin but remember it is a fight that will last as long as you remain in the body. You shall be made conquerors at death but not before.

But how does the Spirit help? – my text confines me to speak chiefly of one way, by helping us to pray. This is[3]:

4. Maketh intercession for us, or in us
That is, he undertakes our concern, manages our cause, indites our prayers, teaches us what to ask and puts life into our frozen hearts so that we ask with some earnestness. On this point:

4.1 Distinguish between the intercession of Christ and of the Spirit
Jesus pleads by his blood before the throne. The Spirit's office is not to plead for us before God but to enable us to plead for ourselves in such a manner as becomes us. Jesus is our advocate in heaven. He has all blessings in his hands ready to bestow on those that ask him. The Spirit is our prompter, that stirs up our hearts to lay hold of the golden opportunity, teaches us to order our cause and fills our mouths with arguments.

4.2 Enquire in what way this is done
In general he does it all by his presence with the soul. Where the Spirit of the Lord is there is liberty – but his presence, like the sun, has various effects and does many things at once (compare *winter* with *spring*). He is therefore represented as performing various offices:

(i) Revealing (1 Cor 2.10; John 16.14)

Our hearts are dull and backward to pray but when the Spirit shows us a glimpse of the things of Christ, of the glories of heaven, of the peace, honour and happiness of the Lord's people, this quickens us. This is like the good wine (Sol. Song 7.9).

(ii) Remembrancing

How forgetful are we, but the promise is fulfilled (John 14.26). We often approach the throne of grace, dumb, and are unwilling to go because we think we have nothing to say – rather dragged by conscience than drawn by love. Yet when at length we try to begin how sweetly is one want, promise, blessing, after another brought to our minds so that at last we are as loath to leave off as we were at first to begin.

(iii) Sealing

Not only showing us the things but helping us to see our interest in them. It is this peculiar application that over-powers our infirmities and makes prayer lively indeed (2 Sam. 7.18). Then if the soul had a hundred tongues it could employ them all.

Now from hence:

1. How much is their ignorance to be pitied who think religion a dull and uncomfortable service. To have access by the blood of Jesus into the holiest of all, to have the Spirit of God discovering to us those things which eye hath not seen and emboldening us to ask the greatest blessings which God can bestow – is this uncomfortable? Can you for shame put the perishing pleasures of sin in competition with these?

2. But there is another mistake [as] some account it – vain and false – madness and enthusiasm. This is urged:

2.1 By the open profane – and they will hardly listen to a serious answer. In brief you will hardly be able to prove that we are *mad* to your own satisfaction. And till you do, it will be easy for us to prove that you are mad yourselves – to venture your everlasting all upon so great an uncertainty, or rather when probabilities are so strongly against.

2.2 By persons of a religious character. But do not such read their Bibles, and have you not heard there of peace and joy in the Holy Ghost – of being satisfied as with marrow and fatness – of being mounted up with wings as eagles? If your religion knows nothing of these things why are you so fond of it, so hard to be persuaded that it is false?

3. But let not the poor mourning souls be discouraged and think, if this is to pray, I never prayed at all. There is another clause in my text added chiefly for your sakes. Of which hereafter.

In the meantime be thankful. Have you not known this Spirit as a Revealer – a Remembrancer? Continue waiting and he will in good time be your Sealer.

CHAPTER FOUR

verse 26 (4)

Likewise the Spirit also helpeth our infirmities: for we know not what we should pray for as we ought: but the Spirit itself maketh intercession for us with groanings which cannot be uttered.

When those who are young in Christian experience hear of the assistance of the Spirit in prayer and how powerfully and certainly he works against all the infirmities of his people, they are apt too hastily to conclude that they know nothing of his operations. They think what they find in themselves is entirely different from what it would be if they were indeed favoured with his assistance.

Again, there are some, who because they have a flow of words and a readiness of expression often at command, are apt to mistake this for a certain evidence of the Spirit's assistance. Without doubt the Spirit, by giving a near and powerful sense of eternal things, does greatly assist us in expressions at some times, yet feeling and speaking are not so closely joined but they may be separated. We are therefore favoured with a more sure mark in my text of the grace of prayer equally suited to encourage the fearful and to repress the confidence of those who lay more stress upon the outward gift than upon the inward affection. I am therefore to speak of the earnestness and mystery of the Spirit's assistance in prayer:

5. With groanings that cannot be uttered

5.1 Groaning
The constant effect of two contending powers is violence and struggle. Observe the course of a river – while nothing resists

it, it glides away with a smooth and gentle stream – but if it meets with a bank or rock in its passage its appearance is altered – it rises and swells and foams and forces its way with a great noise. So a fire will burn quietly while supplied with proper fuel, but if you throw water upon it, there will be immediately a contortion between them which will continue till either the fire or the water is destroyed by its opposite. In like manner, if the stream of holy affections in the soul met with no resistance, if the fire the Spirit kindles in our hearts was not checked and opposed by our remaining corruptions which stifle and damp its influence, there would not be so much groaning in our exercises of prayer. The comfort is that the stream of this river that makes glad the city of God, though it is opposed, cannot be overpowered – this heavenly flame, though it be damped cannot be extinguished but will work its way and prove victorious over all resistance. In the meantime the flesh striveth against the Spirit and the Spirit against the flesh so that there is a groaning.

(i) The Spirit, in helping us to pray, gives us a view of ourselves – leads us backwards to our lives – brings past things to our remembrance – inwards to our hearts – shows us, as Ezekiel 8.13-15, one chamber within another – more and greater abominations than we were aware of. This is a profitable sight but, far from pleasing, it cannot be viewed without much groaning. The Apostle speaks his own experience of this point. Hark how loud he groans (Rom. 7.24).

(ii) The Spirit shows us from the word something of the Divine purity and of the beauty of holiness – in order to teach us what to pray for – but then a comparison of what we are with what we ought to be makes us groan earnestly. So Job groaned (chapter 42.6) – I abhor myself etc..

(iii) The Spirit gives an affecting view of the sufferings of Christ. And will not the groans of a Saviour cause those to sympathise with him who believe or at least hope he groaned and bled for them? Yes, this above anything makes sin appear exceedingly sinful. Then the innumerable defects attending the believer's faith, love and obedience pierce him to the heart. The soul is in Peter's case – one look of love from the Lord Jesus as suffering for his sins brings all his ingratitude to mind at once.

(iv) The Spirit helps the believer to look forward to the accomplishment of the promises – how sweet, glorious and comfortable the prospect when sin shall be subdued and every desire satisfied. But still it is a distant prospect (Prov. 13.12). This stirs up groanings. The language of the soul is Canticles 5.8.

(v) While the Spirit is helping our infirmities he still permits the contrary principle to act in a greater or less degree and even in our most spiritual frames we find causes of groaning from:

(a) Temptations
When we are aiming to lay hold of the promises, the enemy is suffered to come in with – What if these things should not be true? – or – What if you have no right in them? Or perhaps he attacks us with a swarm of black wicked blasphemous thoughts. How does the soul groan to be thus hindered and disappointed, when it was just going to take the prizes.

(b) Our own hearts
Perhaps for a little minute we are closely engaged but presently our hearts start aside like a deceitful

bow and wander with the fool's eyes to the end of the earth. And when we recollect we find that we had strongly forgot where we were or what we were about. This fills us with shame and confusion of face and makes us groan.

(vi) Add to all this what we suffer from the cares, fears, pains, griefs which are inseparable from mortality and cannot be laid wholly aside but will have their share in our thoughts. And it is no wonder, that not withstanding the Spirit's assistance, our prayers should be attended with many and deep groans.

5.2 Which cannot be uttered

We have a character of these groans. *They* cannot *be uttered*. We may understand this two ways:

(i) We cannot give an account of them to others, and that:

(a) For want of confidence

There are many things pass in a believer's heart, when under the Spirit's influence he is brought to a throne of grace, which he could not entrust to the dearest friend upon earth. To the Lord we can confess all but not to men. They could not bear with us. So far as they have experienced the same things perhaps they could, but not beyond that. Now it is the property of a gracious soul to think no heart so bad as his own. Besides in many cases it would not be proper. A communication of experiences is exceedingly helpful if rightly managed, but not of all things nor to all persons. There are some particulars that are best to be kept between God and our own souls.

(b) For want of expressions

If you have had much acquaintance with soul exercises, I question not but you have had some, that you could not relate to your friends if you was ever so willing. And indeed it is common, when believers are desirous to make it known, to stop short and say – Alas I cannot tell you a hundredth part. Sometimes when these seasons are over, we wonder at ourselves, how we found such words. We could not do anything like it if we were to try again. Nor is it strange, for they were not own words but the fruits of the Spirit's intercession for us. Or:

(ii) We cannot distinctly utter them to the Lord.

We found something too big for words – our sense of sin, our desires for grace, our breathings after pardon and holiness, our hungerings and thirstings for a blessed immortality, were such as exceeded all we could say. Or our distress and humiliation was so great that we could say nothing, but only throw ourselves at his feet and sigh and groan before him.

I hope this account will encourage some distressed souls and convince you that you are not so destitute of the Spirit's assistance in prayer as you have been ready to imagine. If I have described something of your experience, and if [what] I have said is agreeable to the scripture, may you be enabled to take the comfort and to give the Lord the glory. If you cannot speak much, you can groan and your groanings are not hid from him. He needs not words to be informed how it is with you. He is the *Searcher of hearts* as in the next verse.

And you that have more liberty in prayer and find it easy to say many things, examine whether you are acquainted with this groaning prayer. The finest composed prayers in the world without these affections are but as a body without a soul. If the stream runs with little difficulty or opposition you have reason to suspect there is more of nature in it than of grace.

It may be proper to remind those who are called out to public prayer, of a temptation we are liable to upon this head. We are apt to be afraid before we attempt to pray before our fellow worms and to be very solicitous afterwards, how we have performed. But there is another question much more important. How have our hearts prayed? How have our inward desires corresponded with our expressions? If we were more intent upon this than upon the other we should not be so backward to improve the gift that God has given us to the edification of his people, nor so easily lifted up or cast down upon the review of our performances.

In a word if we would do anything to purpose let us pray and strive for the help of this promised Spirit, who will surely be afforded to all who seek him. We shall be enabled to watch and pray, to strive, fight and endure and ere long our feeble prayers shall be changed into songs of everlasting praise: To him that has loved us _____

CHAPTER FIVE

verse 27 (1)

*And he that searcheth the hearts knoweth what is the mind
of the Spirit, because he maketh intercession for the saints
according to the will of God.*

It would greatly encourage us in prayer to have a well grounded
hope that our feeble petitions are accepted and shall be surely
answered. For want of this we are at times almost disheart-
ened from praying at all. A fear that our prayers are in vain
arises sometimes from the Lord's delaying to answer just in
our way and at our time. The soul that is[has] been praying
long for a sense of pardon, for assurance of faith or a greater
liberty from indwelling sin and does not find these desires
remarkably fulfilled, is ready to give up and say – He regards
the prayers of his people, but not mine. Surely I am not one of
them. To what purpose then shall I call upon God? Sometimes it arises from the consideration how weak and unworthy our prayers are. The Lord hears them not and how can I
expect he should? I talk of praying, but alas I can only cry and
chatter like a dove. I have no words, no arguments. I can only
offer a few tears and sighs and broken groans that cannot be
uttered. Comfort is provided in my text against both these
complaints. Though the Lord seem to delay he will answer
the requests that are agreeable to his own mind and will, and
though you cannot fully express your own wants, you shall
not therefore fail of anything that is truly good for you. He
knows your state and case exactly, for he searcheth the heart.

1. The title or character – *He that searcheth the heart*.

2. The encouragement therein – *He knoweth what is the mind of the Spirit*.

3. The reason – *because he maketh intercession according to the will of God*.

4. The persons in whom the Spirit makes intercession – *the saints*.

1. The title: He that searcheth the heart
This may well suffice for the subject of one discourse.

1.1 The heart
The whole soul with all its powers and faculties. The understanding, will, affections, the springs and motives of all our actions and conduct – all are included in the heart. It is deep, deceitful and desperately wicked. The thoughts of the heart are innumerable, its contrivances and disguises exceeding many. It is unknown to men, in a great measure unknown to itself, but not so to the Lord.

But the heart sometimes signifies the begun image of God, the work of grace in the soul. Then it is called the new heart, in distinction from the old. The thoughts, desires and workings of this heart likewise are exceeding various, but they are all known to him. In both senses the Lord rules and governs and therefore is styled[4]:

1.2. He that searches, examines – tries, proves as Jeremiah 17.10. This he vindicates as his own prerogative – and our Lord Jesus in the human nature claiming the same privilege (Rev. 2.23) is a full and sufficient proof that he is indeed God over all blessed for ever. The expression implies:

(i) Perfect knowledge

Man indeed may search and be disappointed or mistaken. But when the all wise God makes the scrutiny, what can deceive or escape him? All things are naked and open to him with whom we have to do (Heb. 4.12. Psalm 139.2).

(ii) Continual attention

He not only knows but regards, enquires, searches. He does not behold us with the indifference of a mere spectator but as one with whom we have to do.

(iii) A certain design

If a man will not make diligent search without a purpose in view, much less the Lord. He has indeed told us with what design he searches (Jer. 17.10).

Let us then review these points with application to ourselves. The Lord searches the hearts of:

1. *The self righteous*

Such know not themselves but they are well known to the Lord. Jacob deceived his father by wearing Esau's garments, but the Lord cannot be deceived. He looks through all your outward performance to the heart. A solemn outside, a form of godliness, will not impose upon him (see Malachi 1.14). Is the desire of your hearts to him and does his love lead you to obedience? How are your tempers? Are you lowly in your own eyes, gentle, peaceable – is it your endeavour to do all as you would be done?

2. *Those who live in sin*

2.1 The Lord knows all that you have done and all that is in your hearts. Shame makes you put on some constraint before men but he sees you just as you are.

2.2 He views you with attention. He is about your path, your bed – he observes you in the shop and in the chamber, in the house and in the field, when alone and when in company. He not only notices your idle[5], profane, wicked words and actions but the workings of your thoughts. All the pride, anger, malice, blasphemy, deceit that enters your mind, as fast as it rises is set down in his book.

2.3 For why? To render to you according to your works. He will bring all these secret things into judgment. Sure then it is time to think. See how your case is described (Psalm 7.11-13). Have you a refuge? There is none but Jesus.

3. Mourning souls

You that sigh and groan and cannot speak. Take comfort in this:

3.1 The Lord knows all your wants, even those that you cannot express (Matt. 6.32).

3.2 He has a tender concern about them. This was the Psalmist's comfort (40.17). See how the Lord represents this (Jer. 31.18). Ephraim did not know this.

3.3 He will surely answer. See what a promise to those that groan (Psalm 12.5).

1.3 The methods he takes

That the Lord searches the heart may signify not only his knowledge but the methods he takes to bring us to the knowledge of ourselves. And here chiefly three instruments:

(i) His word – read or preached
There is a majesty and power in this well suited to search

and lay open the heart (Psalm 119.130; see 1 Cor. 14.25). It often begins in this way. It causes wonder – a person begins to see or to imagine that there is something more in the word of God or the preaching of the gospel than they were aware of.

(ii) His Spirit

This brings something home to their hearts with a particular application, which calls off their thoughts from others and makes them busy at home. As if one of you was attending a trial at Assize and while you were eager listening to the cause and thought yourself safe, the judge should keep his eye fixed upon you, at last mention your name aloud and say, Stop that person. The law has a demand against him. He must stand a trial with the rest and if he is cast he dies. Would not this surprise – especially if you suddenly call to remembrance something long past and forgot that exposed you to the rigour of the law? Something like this it is when the Spirit brings the word close to the heart and says, Thou art the man.

(iii) His providence

This generally falls in with the other two when a sinner begins to be convinced. Some outward thing commonly happens to fix the dart the deeper, to enflame their corruptions, to open a door for Satan's temptations. And thus the Lord searches and discovers to them the evil of their hearts, takes away all their vain excuses, so that they have not the shadow of a hope left but what lies in his free mercy.

Is not this the experience of some? Take encouragement – you are wounded, but it is the Lord has done it – and he who has wounded will heal. There is precious balm and a compassionate Physician.

CHAPTER SIX

verse 27 (2)

And he that searcheth the hearts knoweth what is the mind of the Spirit, because he maketh intercession for the saints according to the will of God.

We have spoken of the Lord's character here – the *Searcher of hearts*. This title is like the cloud between the Egyptians and Israel. It is full of darkness and terror to careless sinners and formal worshippers – but it affords comfort to sincere and humble souls. Let us consider:

2. The encouragement: He knoweth what is the mind of the Spirit

He knoweth. The word has two senses. He is acquainted with it and he accepts and approves it. The word *mind* the same as verse 6 – the savour, inclination, desire and tendency of the believing heart is well known and graciously accepted by the *Searcher of hearts*, notwithstanding the defects and infirmities that cloud and defile their best services. Now this is a comfortable thought to gracious souls.

2.1 With regard to their own secret exercises

(i) They are sensible of their defect and inability with regard to the whole compass of prayer. Their sins are innumerable and so are their wants. They have a great many causes of praise, many sweet subjects for their prayers, precepts, promises and discoveries opened in the word of God. They would willingly attend to them all but they cannot. They still forget something which they would wish to remember. Their confessions, acknowledgements and petitions are all too general, and if they were only to be answered according to their own prayers they would come short of many blessings. But the Searcher knows all – he knows the *mind*, that though they cannot bring out every particular as they would wish, yet the best of their desire is towards himself. They long to mourn over their sins with greater freedom. They would willingly seek to him for every good they need. This he knows and deals with accordingly. He has promised where there is a willing mind to accept according to what he gives, to do more than we can either ask or think. We are not straitened in him though we are in ourselves. When our requests are right in the main, he says to us as to Solomon (1 Kings 3): *Because thou hast asked this thing – I have also given thee that which thou hast not asked.*

(ii) They are sensible in many particulars of their own ignorance and unfitness to choose. If the Lord was to give us all our desires we should suffer more than we do. Of many he sees and says, ye know not what ye ask. And when this is the case, though he will always approve himself a God that heareth prayer in the end, yet for the present he will disappoint us. He regards *the mind of the Spirit* rather than the sound of the words and will do that which is best for our interest and his own glory, though our misapprehensions should look another way. Perhaps we want the thing *now*. He sees it best for us to *wait*. He refuses us something we ask to give us something better. He baulks us in the means we depend much on, that we may in good time receive the blessing more immediately and more clearly from himself.

(iii) They are sensible of evil mixing with their best things, which make them ready to say, Alas will the Lord regard such prayers as mine? But he knows the mind of the Spirit

– that though evil is present with us, our aim is to the good, that we do not (if believers) pray in our own strength nor expect to be heard in our names. He therefore beholds us (according to the mind of our spirit) in Jesus the beloved. For his sake he passes by our unworthiness and receives us graciously.

2.2 With regard to the judgment of men

(i) The world is a hard judge of the people of God – ready to make the most of every mistake and fault they may at times be drawn into. And when they can find no just objection against them, they will not stick to invent false ones and lay to their charge things that they never knew. Yes, if you are setting out in the Lord's way, you must expect to bear this cross – to be called madmen, hypocrites. They will watch for your halting and if you give them the least advantage they will put everything in the worst light it will possibly bear. Let this urge you to a close dependence on the Lord. Pray that you may be led and kept because of your observers and enabled to maintain a conscience void of offence. Then how comfortable will it be to appeal from their malice to him who searches your heart, and he knows the frame and mind of your spirit (2 Sam. 7.20). *Let them curse – but bless thou.*

(ii) You will need this retreat likewise even in your converse with your brethren the Lord's children. You will find none that has all that tenderness, compassion and skill which your case requires. Though our infirmities and trials seem sufficient to soften and humble us, they are not so in effect. We must allow that even Christians can deal harshly or speak unadvisedly or else (alas) shall we not *unchristian* ourselves. When we have considered a person long under the character of a sinner or enemy, we are sometimes too

backward in judging favourably a beginning of a change
(Acts 9.13-26). When a professor is fallen we are too ready
at the severe. Indeed we should be open and honest in all
our testimony against sin, but O how much tenderness
should be used by those who rightly consider themselves
and know if they were left to temptation they have no more
of their own than others. Sometimes we mistake and blame
what is truly good as Eli did in Hannah's case. But in all
these respects the soul that is truly sincere may take comfort in appealing to the Lord. Though we may mistake you,
the *Searcher of hearts* knows what is the mind of the Spirit.

2.3 With regard to the accusations of Satan

To him likewise you may cry against the accusations of Satan.
He will perhaps bring heavy charges against you and you
cannot wholly deny them. The tempter always turns accuser
when he can no longer prevail. He will remind you of your
former compliances with his suggestions. He will make you
take notice how much hold he still has in your corrupt nature
and that there is still something within you that listens to him
and would willingly yield. This is the bitterest fruit of
temptations, they discover[6] the vileness of our hearts and we
find inclinations stirring us up to the things that we allow not.
But the Lord knoweth the mind of the Spirit, the new Spirit
which he has given you. He sees that you do not tamely comply,
but set yourself in his strength to fight against the evil. It
therefore shall not be imputed unto you, but to the enemy of
peace who labours to hinder the work of God in your soul. He
shall be rebuked and you shall be delivered.

Let me recommend it as a caution to all. Try your prayers by
this consideration. The Lord knoweth what is the mind of your
spirit.

1. If you use a form – though it be ever so sound, it will not be accepted unless it expresses the desire of your hearts. I have mentioned this before but it needs to be repeated. Some of you perhaps are fond of the Lord's prayer and would think all others good for little unless that was to conclude them. But [have you][7] ever considered what you ought to mean when you repeat? Is God your father? How or when was this relation brought about? If so, where is his reverence? etc..

Remark briefly on each petition.

2. If you use no set form, be not content with a flow of words. Nature may prompt much this way where the exercise of grace is very low. Pass the same judgment on prayer as the Apostle does on preaching (1 Cor. 14.19). Five words, a few broken sentences from a broken and contrite heart, are more desirable than to pray for hours without spiritual feeling – this in the Lord's judgment is like speaking in an unknown tongue. Better to weep with the Publican than to talk with the Pharisee.

3. Lastly, this thought, like every part of scripture doctrine, is suited not only to comfort us under our infirmities, but to humble us from a sense of them. The Lord knows and accepts our poor breathings, but he likewise sees the corrupt mixture with which they are attended. Have you been favoured with liberty and freedom and does Satan endeavour to ensnare you with spiritual pride, to make you think – Surely I am somebody now? To check this temptation, think how much the Lord saw amiss in your best frames – admire his condescension that he will permit such a polluted creature to take his name into your lips and long for a deliverance from this world of sin and sorrow. Long for the hour that shall release you from every impediment and join you with that glorious assembly where their worship is perfectly spiritual. Lord prepare us for the change and hasten it.

CHAPTER SEVEN

verse 27 (3)

*And he that searcheth the hearts knoweth what is the
mind of the Spirit, because he maketh intercession
for the saints according to the will of God.*

When the matter of our petitions are agreeable to the word of
God and when our hearts agree to what our lips pronounced,
this is spiritual prayer. This is a good reason to hope that our
prayers, poor and unworthy as they are, and though attended
with a great mixture of imperfection and wandering, pierce
the clouds, reach the throne of the Most High and shall not be
in vain; but shall surely bring an answer of peace. So we are
taught from the text. He that searcheth – *knoweth*, notices and
approves *because* [*he maketh intercession for the saints*] –
according to the will of God.

This is the point:

3. He maketh intercession according to the will of God

The reason: *Because he maketh etc.*. Let us then for confirma-
tion enquire from the word of God, in what manner it is his
will we should pray – and if we find our prayers run in this
way, we may safely conclude that we are favoured with a
measure of this spirit.

It is his will:

3.1 That we should pray in the name of Jesus.

This is the proper sense of Philippians 2.10. See likewise John
16.26. Now this has a spiritual meaning. It intends something
more than bowing when we hear the name of Christ or
repeating it at the end of our prayers. It supposes a sense of

our utter unworthiness to pray without our advocate, and a persuasion that Jesus is worthy to be heard on our behalf, if he will please to undertake our cause. Now this I am persuaded is the case of every awakened soul.

(i) They know prayer to be a duty and they dare not live without it. Yet guilt and sin makes them cry, Wherewith shall I come before the Lord? If this could not be answered they must sink in despair, but when they hear of Jesus they find his character just suited to their case and therefore they are emboldened to try.

(ii) Though they are subject to doubt his willingness, they are persuaded of his power. Who knows but at last he will show himself favourable and thus, notwithstanding all their fears, they are helped to persevere.

3.2 That spiritual and heavenly things should have the first and prevailing place in our desires (Matt. 6.33).

And here all that are awakened pray according to the will of God. They have many trials and complaints of a worldly kind which they design to spread before the Lord and to cast upon him according to his gracious permission. But the chief things they cry for are the light of his countenance, the power of his grace and the knowledge of his love. Nothing will satisfy them without these. But if they are remarkably answered in these they can contentedly leave the rest with him and say – Let him do as seemeth him good.

3.3 That our prayers should be offered with a real sense of our own defects, sins and unworthiness.

See the pattern (Luke 18.13). Now those who are awakened are convinced of this at all times, but especially when they draw near to God in prayer. They see iniquity in their most holy things etc..

If you pray thus you are certainly in a degree under the influence of the Spirit. You pray according to the will of God and shall surely be answered. For these things are beyond the power and contrary to the inclinations of the natural man.

1. None but those who have the Spirit see the need and worth of Christ (1 Cor. 12.3),
2. Or prefer spiritual blessings to temporal,
3. Or be truly ashamed of their best services. Here is the trial of the self-righteous. They will confess evil in their lives but then they think their prayers will make amends.

4. The Saints
I proposed to speak a little of the persons or the title here given them. They are called *saints*. This word is misunderstood by many.

4.1 With some (so strangely are they averse to the will of God) this name with which the Lord honours his dear children is *a term of reproach*. When they would express their illwill against a person who walks according to the gospel, they think it sufficient to call him a saint. That is they would have it understood a hypocrite, or else a poor dull precise creature who justly deserves their scorn and contempt. But the Lord whom they reproach through the sides[8] of his people will one day arise to plead their cause. Then their enemies shall be ashamed.

4.2 Others appropriate this title to the Apostles and Evangelists, or to a few whose names are in the Almanac – to some of those who are called the fathers – as if it was *a title given to some upon the account of their own superior goodness*. But this title is common to every believer in Jesus. In themselves the best of them are worthy of the name of sinners but from the relation they bear to his love and grace they are all equally worthy of the name of *saints*. So the Lord is pleased to call them and who shall gainsay it? But what is the meaning of the word?

The word in the Old Testament most usually rendered *saint* signifies one who has obtained mercy. Those who have seen their need of mercy and fled to Jesus for it are saints, from the moment they put their trust in him. For all such do and shall obtain mercy of the Lord and in consequence of this they are ready to show mercy unto others.

In the New Testament, *saints* signifies those who are sanctified. And these two senses meet together in every believer. They are justified from their sins by the blood of Jesus and sanctified by his Spirit.

Of these it is said, *The Spirit maketh* intercession in them according to the will of God. Fear not, only believe, though the Lord seem to delay. The prayers which are under the influence of his Spirit and agreeable to his will cannot possibly miscarry.

But you who pray not at all, or who see little need of Jesus, or of the assistance of his Spirit, who think anything but these qualifications can render your prayers pleasing, or those of you whose names are not changed, who do not live or desire to live upon Jesus for justification and sanctification, those who either despise the name of saints or are utter strangers to the thing signified by it – what comfort can I offer to you? Alas, he that searcheth the heart knoweth what is your mind. He views all your sins, sees through all your disguises, and soon you will be stripped of all and stand naked and trembling before him. O consider this, you that forget God. Seek his face and live. Call upon him for this Spirit. Jesus is ready to bestow it upon all that ask. He has obtained it even for the rebellious. So shall you be saved from your guilt and fears and not be ashamed before him at his appearing.

CHAPTER EIGHT

verse 28 (1)

*And we know that all things work together for good
to them that love God, to them who are the called
according to his purpose.*

In this verse the Apostle begins to treat of the third great argument of consolation to the people of God under all their afflictions and infirmities. Great is the comfort arising from a believing view of the glory that shall be revealed, when all our tears shall be wiped away. This he sets before us from verses 17 to 25. Great is the comfort to know that even at present we are not left to suffer and struggle in our own strength, but have the sure promise of his Spirit to help our infirmities and by giving us liberty in prayer, to supply us with strength and grace suited to every time of need – verses 26 to 27. It now gives us a farther ground of support by leading our thoughts to the providence, appointment and purpose of our heavenly father. All our dispensations are under his direction and all intended and overruled by him to work together for our good. What I lately delivered amongst you from Psalm 74.14 may be considered as an illustration of a part of this subject. But it is a large and fruitful point and seems to afford me scope for several discourses without running much into the repetition of what I have formerly observed.

My method will be suggested by the order in which the words lie. And you will easily perceive a great variety of meditations may be drawn from the following heads:

1. Who they are that can say with the Apostle *We know* that all things etc. and by what means they come to know it.

2. To illustrate this truth and prove from scripture and experience *that all things* really do and must *work together for good* to them that love God.

3. To point out what is implied by the expression of *working together*.

4. To enlarge upon the character of those to whom all things etc., *Them that love God.*

5. To consider the vocation or *calling* of the people of God and its sure connection with his eternal *purpose*. This would be an introduction to the deep things contained in the following verses.

1. We Know
It is a common reproach thrown upon vital religion, as if it lay all in high sensible affections, a warmth in the heart without light in the understanding. But indeed the exercise of spiritual affections is founded on solid scriptural knowledge. We cannot believe, obey or rejoice any farther than we know. The cause of our many complaints is chiefly our ignorance. But a measure of real spiritual knowledge is given to every child of God and by this the meanest and weakest of them is wiser than the wisest man in the world who lives without God. Perhaps they know nothing of languages or history, have little of the knowledge of the world that puffeth up, but they know the plague of their own hearts. They know the way of salvation etc.. Amongst other things they know that all things work together for good.

But let us enquire more particularly:

1.1 Who they are that know this

(i) We are sure that those who are governed by what they call their reason, who judge according to the sight of their eyes and after the hearing of their ears, do not know it. Those who are governed by outward appearances only will judge the direct contrary. Because the Lord's people are an afflicted people they count them unhappy; but they bless the covetous whom the Lord abhorreth. They will despise a Lazarus and little imagine that his dunghill and his sores can work for his good and would be glad to change places with such as are clothed in purple and fine linen and fare sumptuously, without stopping to enquire whether their riches are a blessing to them or a curse. An increase of goods is the object of their desire. They think nothing but success and pleasure can work for their good and if they are afflicted and brought low, they neither expect nor desire that their crosses should prove blessings.

(ii) Neither can those who have merely a head knowledge of scripture truth be said to know this truly, though they may own it in words. There is little difference only in talk between these and the others. They are as prone to envy those above them and to slight those below them, as uneasy and rebellious when the Lord touches them close as if they believed just contrary to what they profess.

(iii) Those only truly know it, who feel its influence and power reconciling them to all the dispensations of God. David proved that he knew it when he took Shimei's reviling so patiently. Joseph knew it when he so tenderly reminded his brethren of their fault, as if he would in a manner wholly clear them (Gen. 45.5). Paul knew it when he said, None of these things move me. I am ready not only to be bound but also to die. In like manner if you know this, you find these effects of your knowledge:

(a) It humbles you under the hand of God and enables you to say – The cup which my Father has put in my hand, shall I not drink it?

(b) It takes away your anger and resentment against men. You cannot be very angry if you believe that whether they intend it or not, they are working your good.

(c) It gives you courage to press on in the path of duty, notwithstanding difficulties and dangers may seem to stand in your way – for why should you fear them, if you are sure beforehand that they will work for your good?

Only in judging of yourself in these respects, be thankful for finding yourselves thus disposed, though the degree of your attainment is but small, and do not say you know nothing at all of it because you find a contrary principle warring within you.

1.2 By what means they came to know it
For it is a wisdom acquired and not born with them.

(i) The Lord by his Spirit has enlightened their understandings to know wherein their true good consists. By nature we are apt to seek our good in the things relating to the body – such as health, riches, honours. Now so long as this mistake continues it is impossible to believe that sickness, poverty and disgrace can work for good. But the soul that is taught by the word and Spirit of God, knows that its true good does not consist in health or wealth or life itself, but in the favour of God, in holiness and in those spiritual blessings which are only known to those who receive, and is therefore well satisfied that whatever is a means of advancing sanctification and bringing the soul to nearer communion and greater conformity with God is indeed working for good.

(ii) They learn it from scripture that the Lord always has in fact overruled all things to work together for good to his people. To confirm us in this was one great design (we may think) in recording the lives and experiences of the saints of old. They were sometimes so pressed that they cried, All these things are against me. But the event showed that the Lord was carrying on his purpose of love to them by those very things which they found fault with. Now those who love God, love his word. They are led to study it and thus they are made wise and attain to know that all things work and shall work together for their good.

(iii) They learn it by experience. They are perhaps much at a loss to account for the present dispensation and ready to say – Could not I have without this trial? This is their infirmity. But if they look back to some distance of time, then they clearly perceive that all things, even those that were grievous, have worked for good. Remember believer that dark trying hour – was it not hard to bear – yet now you are sensible the Lord had a gracious design in it. If he had not visited you with sickness or distress, if he had not laid his hand upon your idol, or taken away the desire of your eyes with a stroke, perhaps you had still been in your sins – at least you could not have known so much of his faithfulness, power and love. You would have missed many proofs you have had that he is a God hearing prayer – and of the sweetness and truths of his promises.

Inference:

1. Be persuaded then believers to trust that God whom you have so often tried and found faithful. Why are you still questioning him at every new turn?

2. Do any desire an experimental knowledge of this? Remember the Lord Jesus is the great teacher. It is in and from him you must seek the ground and reason of spiritual truth. Think of what he has done and suffered for his people and you will not wonder that all things work for their good.

3. We know by the same scripture that this blessing is restrained to them that love God. If you love him not, the contrary to this is true. All things speak to you not good but evil.

CHAPTER NINE

verse 28 (2)

*And we know that all things work together for good
to them that love God, to them who are the
called according to his purpose.*

Every true believer can in some measure say, *We know this* –
but there is a great difference even in the best between their
settled persuasion in judgment and their experimental knowledge. If we knew this as we ought to know it, many of our
complaints and fears would cease. May the Lord bless what I
shall say to increase our certainty and assurance of this comfortable truth.

2. All things work together for good

I propose to illustrate and prove it from scripture and experience that all things work together for good. He has not only
taught in his word but has shown us in various instances and
teaches his people each one in their own concerns that they
actually do so. We may range the all things a believer meets
with into this threefold division:

1. the dispensations that are immediately from God
2. the temptations of Satan and
3. the conduct of men towards us

2.1. Dispensations from God are of two sorts:

(i) Spiritual
Now you will readily allow that the bright and comfortable manifestation of his presence works for good to those
that love him – the difficulty is to conceive how the con-

trary should do so. He sometimes seems to act as an enemy. He leads them into darkness, gives them a sense of his terrors so that they complain. He covers himself with a cloud and shuts out their prayers. But even this is amongst the all. It is thus he leads them more into an acquaintance of their own hearts, teaches them more highly to value his smiles, to be more fearful of abusing them, stirs them up to greater wrestling and earnestness in prayer and gives them more admiring and affecting views of the freedom and power of his grace. (So Hos. 2.14; Ps. 42; Job 23.10; Prov. 30.8-11.)

(ii) Providential

We are not so apt to be afraid of favourable providences, though indeed the danger is equal or greater here – but when the Lord breaks our cisterns, blasts our designs, sends a worm to the root of our gourd, takes away health, substance, friends, can this work for good? You have heard of Job and seen the end he obtained of the Lord – let his history be instead of a thousand. Was not his a heavy case, yet did not things work together for his good at last? Farther I appeal to yourselves, I would lead you back to the time when you said, The evil I feared is come upon me. And now – what harm has it done you, if you love the Lord? Was not it a means of showing you the vanity of the creature, of quickening you when your hearts were cleaving to the dust? Did it not give you a proof, which otherwise you would not have had, of the all sufficiency of God, and has not this and other things of the kind, made you at times to say with David – O that I had wings like a dove – to fly to that blessed world where trouble shall never enter?

2.2 Satan's temptations, are either when he assaults us:

(i) Openly as a liar, and works upon our guilt and corruptions to terrify us into despair, or

(ii) Secretly as a serpent, when he would entice us to wander from the paths of peace and to sin against our good God. This is a tender point to speak of, yet the word of God and experience shows these things work for his people's good – no thanks to Satan whose purpose is to destroy, no thanks to our evil rebellious hearts. The praise is wholly to him who by his power and wisdom can bring good out of evil.

As to the first – the fierce accusations of Satan make us more sensible of the need and value of mercy – beat us off from all vain pleas and false hopes, confirm to us the power and reality of invisible things, give us a soft and sympathising spirit to others and teach us how to speak to them.

As to the other, his constant tempting to evil is a means of keeping the believer more constantly upon his guard and especially when he has prevailed. Then there is true grace in the heart, when the Lord heals the breach – what shame, what indignation, what godly sorrow. Witness David (Ps. 51). Witness Peter.

2.3 As to dealings of men

How all their counsels and designs work together, how the Lord gives his people favour when it is necessary and overrules the plots of their enemies to bring about that good which he intends them, you may clearly see in the remarkable instance of Joseph – and how he manages them for his church, see in the case of Esther.

But these examples, where a variety of interfering design all issue and centre in the good of them that love God, remind me of the expression

3. Together

None of these things singly, but all of them together. As in the arch of a bridge we cannot say of any single stone this supports the *arch*, but each one in his place, and all unite so in the whole, that if one was taken away or wanting, the whole arch would fall. So in the growth of the corn, we cannot say it is the sun without the wind, the wind without the rain, or rain without the sun. All are equally needful in the proper seasons and places and out of their proper seasons would do more harm than good. So the church and each believer is God's building, God's husbandry. He prepares and times and directs every circumstance – not all comfort lest they should be lifted, not all trouble lest they should be cast down. He will magnify his strength in their weakness – therefore he lets them feel their weakness. He will show himself great in saving them from their enemies – therefore he lets their enemies try what they can do. He will have them hate sin, therefore he lets them sometimes smart for it. He will have them tender-hearted to others, therefore lets them suffer themselves. He would have them weary of earth and therefore embitters earthly things to them – but in the end he makes all work for good.

Hence:
1. See the privilege of the believer

(i) His honour
We account a person to be great when many hands are employed for him – but a child of God is in this respect above a king – every person, providence and circumstance of his life are working for his good. The instruments are

divers – they know not each others' intentions, yea they may have opposite intentions yet all meet in the same point. As in the movement of a watch the several parts are made by different hands, each attends to his own work without thinking of the rest – and the chief workman assigns each his proper place according to his own design. So all the several parts of a believer's experience are fitted to each other. There is a dependence and relation amongst all the wheels and springs and the Lord puts them together, sets them agoing and from the whole produces a marvellous work, the complete salvation of his people, to the glory of his own name.

(ii) His safety
What [can] possibly harm him when even his enemies are constrained to work for his good?

2. If any are capable of abusing this doctrine they are not those in my text – *they do not love God*. Those who love will hate evil – and they know though he can bring good of it, they shall have cause to mourn.

3. Is not this encouragement to seek the love of God? Without it nothing can do you good – with it nothing can harm you. Seek then the knowledge of Christ.

CHAPTER TEN

verse 28 (3)

*And we know that all things work together for
good to them that love God, to them who are
the called according to his purpose.*

At the first reading of this promise, it would be no wonder if
all that hear it should be ready to claim an interest in it. For
who is so abandoned as to make an open public profession
that he does not love God? The greatest offence and displeas-
ure a faithful minister can possibly give to unawakened hearers is to touch them closely upon this point. They will bear to
be told that they are sinners in general, yea perhaps you may
speak of their particular sins, charge them to their faces with
their drunkenness, lying, swearing etc., and come off toler-
ably well, but if you attempt to show them that they are *enemies* to God, that their hearts are full of black enmity against
the God that made them, this will provoke their pride to the
uttermost. But the case is otherwise with such as are truly
awakened – these see so much evil in themselves and such
inexpressible excellence in God as manifested in his Son, that
perhaps long after his love has touched their hearts and enkin-
dled their affections towards him, they can hardly be persuaded
that they love him at all. I have endeavoured to prove both
these points separately in the course of these lectures and I
shall now take them together in speaking to:

4. Them that love God
The character of those to whom this and every promise in the
Bible is made: *Them that love God*. I cannot enlarge on this
without at the same time describing those who love him not,

that is who hate him, for there is no medium, no such thing as standing neuter, in a state of indifference between love and hatred towards him.

Now those who love God:

1. Can give reasons why they love him.
2. Give evidences that they do love him

4.1 They give reasons *why*.

(i) One we have (1 John 4.19). It does not mean that none love him who have not a strong persuasion and manifestation of his love to them sensibly shed abroad in their hearts – for then our state would be as changeable as our frames. For many who have for a season rejoiced in his love have lived to walk in darkness and to sink almost into despair. But it implies:

(a) An acknowledgement, that the love we bear him (such as it is) is not of our own natural stock, but arises from the Lord's love to us, in opening our eyes and softening our hearts.

(b) A spiritual understanding to know and rejoice in the work of redemption. O, says the soul, when I think what God has done to make the salvation of sinners consistent with his own glory – when I think of his sending his Son, when I think of Jesus wounded and bleeding, dying for sin, when I see many who were once afar off brought nigh by the power of this grace – the thought rejoices my heart and though my own hopes are very small and faint, yet I see such a beauty and excellence in this lover of souls that I feel my desires drawn forth towards him. I long to love him better and I abhor myself that I love him no more. If you can say this, you certainly love God and the promise is yours.

(ii) Another reason is Psalm 116.1,2. Those who love God have known their need of him. They have found trouble and sorrow; they have been in distress from which they were sensible none but he could deliver them. This has made them call unto him, O Lord I beseech thee deliver my soul, and if not quite relieved, they see it owing to his mercy and power that they are out of hell. Therefore they say, I love the Lord because he has heard my voice and supplication.

(iii) Another reason is the excellency and suitableness they see in him. Before they were hesitating, looking for happiness here and there, but now their choice is fixed. Thus it was with Peter when he said, Lord, to whom shall we go!

Now will those who see nothing wonderful in redeeming love, nothing desirable in communion with God, who account it a weariness and burden to call on him in prayer, will these pretend to love him? On the contrary they certainly hate and despise him in their hearts. The brightest display of his wisdom is foolishness in their eyes etc..

4.2 They give evidences that they do love him.
Their affections work in the same way towards God as the affections of natural men work towards worldly objects.

(i) When we love a person, we delight in their company. It is pleasant to be near to those whom we dearly love. And thus the soul that is taught to love the Lord can say – It is good for me to draw near unto God. O how I long for greater nearness. Lord, lift up the light of thy countenance.

(ii) In absence, a letter or news from those we love is welcome. Thus the soul that loves God loves his word, loves his ordinances, loves to hear his ministers speaking largely of his goodness and beauty.

(iii) We love the friends of those we love and for their sakes. When the love of God prevails, there is a general love and goodwill to all creatures as his workmanship – but especially to his children who bear his image. These, says the loving soul, are in my eyes the excellent of the earth. I esteem the meanest of them before all the great and mighty that know him not.

(iv) Love is always attended with a desire to please. You hardly think anything too much to do for those you dearly love. Therefore if you love God, obedience to his commands is your delight. It is true the defects you find in your best endeavours greatly lessen your pleasure but then you do not complain of his commandments and account them grievous, you do not wish that his rule was less strict. The burthen you groan under arises from the sense you have of your own inability to serve him as you ought. And you would prefer a power to serve him better to thousands of gold and silver and are seeking an increase of this power in the diligent use of the means he has appointed for that purpose. If you can stand this test, you are a Christian.

(v) If the person you love is at a distance you feel a desire to be with him. So if you love God your thoughts will be going forth, looking within the veil to where Jesus is. You will at times feel a desire to see him in his glory. Here some will be discouraged again and say, Alas, the thoughts of death terrify me. This makes me think I love him not, for when I look to the solemn hour of my appearance before him I tremble. I answer though your faith is of the right sort, yet if weak, you may be afraid of dying – that is of the pain, sickness, distraction and temptations which are often the forerunners of death – and perhaps you fear because your evidences are not strong. But then when you consider that after death you shall sin no more, that when you see Jesus you shall be perfectly like him and forever with him, does not this make you say, O if I knew my sins were pardoned, if I could but believe that he would meet me in the dark valley, how gladly would I welcome the summons and shut my eyes upon all here to open them in his presence? I am weary of this dull round, eating and drinking, sinning and repenting. I shall never be well till I get safe to that land where nothing enters that defileth.

Such as these are the evidences of love – those who feel such dispositions towards God as manifested in the gospel undoubtedly love him. And in the same way we may prove that many love him not [at] all. Yea their hearts are set against him.

1. Many delight not in God nor seek after him as their portion. They have chosen their own idols and devices. They say not, O that I knew where I could find him, but if they can enjoy the perishing pleasures of sin, would willingly shut him out of their thoughts.

2. Therefore they slight or abuse the means in which he makes himself known. They will not seek him by prayer, they let his word lie neglected by, they put no value upon his preached gospel, or if they attend upon outward means it is for form's sake. They have no relish or blessing in what they do.

3. They show that they love him not because they have no love to his people. These things go together (1 John 5.1).

4. If love expresses a desire to please and a fear to offend – what a plea can those have who live in the contempt and breach

of his commandments? Not a few who imitate the children of God in other things must be shut out by this trial. Perhaps you may have a form of godliness, may profess yourself a great friend to the gospel and crowd yourself amongst the children, but if you live in the practice of any one known sin you have no ground to hope that you have any part or lot in the matter. They that love the Lord hate evil.

5. Nor can such have any desire after heaven, as described in the scripture. If the Lord would give you your desires upon earth he might keep heaven to himself. Does the heart of any say so? Then be sure you love him not. And how should you when your inclinations and will are directly contrary to his!

And what will become of you if you die without the love of God? See 1 Corinthians 13. O that you perceived the want of it. This would lead you to Jesus. He is able to give it to you. Consider how he has loved sinners. May his Spirit enable you to love him again or else: 1 Corinthians 16.22.

You that have these marks of love though in a low degree, fear not – he will not despise the day of small things or quench the smoking flax. All things shall work together for your good. Your love to him shall sweeten all your difficulties, his love to you shall enable you to hold out, make you more than conquerors in the end and bestow on you the crown of life which the Lord has promised to them that love him and wait for his appearing.

CHAPTER ELEVEN

verse 28 (4)

*And we know that all things work together for good
to them that love God, to them who are
the called according to his purpose.*

Promise a recapitulation of the former heads and proceed to:

5. Them who are called according to his purpose
The vocation or calling of God's people and its sure, sure connection with his eternal purpose.

With this clause the Apostle enters upon the last and highest ground of consolation to the people of God. His other arguments are taken from points of which they have some experience in themselves, but now he leads them out of themselves to the rock that is higher than they. He leads their thoughts back to before the foundation of the world was laid, he leads them forward to beyond the bounds of time and sense and shows that from everlasting to everlasting the Lord had one certain design in favour of his people which he cannot, will not, miss. And this stands as a proper conclusion to the affection in the beginning of the verse that all things shall work together for good to them that love God – nor can it be maintained without it, for if anything could happen to them without or beside the purpose of God concerning them, it might be justly questioned whether that could work together for their good or no.

Having therefore coasted as it were thus far along the shore, we must soon launch forth into the deep, I trust not without a good pilot – for we shall take the word of God with us. The two following verses will necessarily call me to the consid-

eration of a subject which I seldom care to meddle with in a
direct way. Not because I think it hard to prove the doctrine of
God's sovereign grace from scripture, or to show its consist-
ence with Christian experience. Not because I do not believe
it to be a wholesome and comfortable doctrine, tending as our
Article 17[9] assures, to establish faith in Christ and to enkindle
fervent love to God. I believe it to be a doctrine according to
godliness comfortable and wholesome and should not be able
to preach a single sermon with pleasure without keeping it
constantly in view – yet I seldom do more than touch upon it
unless I find it directly in my text for such reasons as these:

1. I observe this is not a point in which the Lord instructs his
people either chiefly or universally. Many of his dear children, from whom in other things I would desire to learn, do,
and will, differ from me in this – and often from the connec-
tions they have been in, they have such a misapprehension
about it and have been so strongly prejudiced against it, that
they can hardly hear of it without being grieved and offended.
And I hope I shall be always unwilling to grieve the weakest
of those who believe in Jesus and keep his commandments.

2. I observe that it is peculiarly true of this doctrine that a man
can receive nothing unless it be given him from heaven.
Though I should deliver my sentiment in the clearest manner
and support it by the fullest proof, I cannot convince you unless you are just in that state and degree of experience in which
the Lord may see fit to give you farther light. Or if I could
persuade you in a way of reasoning to agree with me for the
present, unless you have a deeper sense of the truth than my
words can give you you would gain nothing – you could not
hold it. The next flood of temptation would sweep your new
opinion away. If you are a sincere seeker of the truth as it is in
Jesus, I might leave you to the Lord's teaching. Go on and as

you become more acquainted with your own heart and the power of Satan, we shall be nearer of a mind. A time may probably come when you will find this doctrine which now you are ready to put from you the only refuge that will afford you comfort.

3. I observe with grief the abuse that is made of this point by many who embrace it as a notion in their heads and have not the power and savour of grace in their hearts. So that my controversy, if I have any, will not lie so much with those who differ as with those [who] profess to agree with me, and I speak of it the seldomer because it requires so much caution to manage it aright.

Especially in this place, where perhaps there is hardly a single person who will not stand up for the words election, predestination and final perseverance, but alas how few of those who will contend about holding out to the end, give us satisfactory evidence that they have taken so much as a single step in the way.

Many I know have the presumption to plead God's sovereignty as an excuse for continuing in sin and say, if I am chosen, he will call me in his own time.

But since there are some who find this precious truth to be food and life, joy and strength to their souls, I am not at all unwilling to consider it, now it lies so fairly in my way that I must mention it or desist from my purpose of going through the chapter.

From the clause I am to speak upon we shall enter upon it as it were by degrees and prepare the way to what is laid down more expressly in the two following verses. Let us then as in the presence of God and with a just distrust of our own hearts, lest we profane these high subjects with our manner of speaking or thinking of them, consider these two points:

1. What is the calling here spoken of.
2. That this calling is according to the purpose of God.

5.1 The calling

The Lord's people are often said to be called (1 Cor. 1.2; 1 Pet. 2.9; Jude 1). On this I must be brief the rather as it will offer to be more largely spoken to from verse 30. Observe:

(i) The calling cannot mean the outward preaching of the gospel. The reason is plain in my text. Of this it is said '*Many* are called but few chosen'. And so far are all things from working together for their good, that the very calling they are favoured with, will through their disobedience greatly aggravate both their guilt and their misery.

(ii) The same reason stands against that sort of asking, those hasty and passing convictions, which constrain people for a little season to make a profession from which they afterwards turn aside as a dog to his vomit. It was no advantage to Judas to be thus called, or to Ananias and Sapphira that they were outwardly added to the church. Rather it would be better for such not to have known the way of righteousness than etc. (2 Pet. 2.21).

The calling therefore is:

(a) Spiritual

It is wrought by the Spirit of God and it lays hold of the spirit of the sinner. It is something more than that alarm and uneasiness which is often felt while the sound of the preacher's voice is in the ear and from which people quickly recover as soon as they get into the open air. It is more than a half reformation from a few gross sins. It is the voice of God that brings the law to the conscience and the conscience to the bar (see Heb. 4.12). That cuts off every plea for hope and brings the soul into the state of a trembling prisoner till a way of escape is opened by the knowledge of Christ.

(b) It is effectual
It changes the heart, the views, the affections and the practices. So that the persons called differ as much from their former selves as they can do from anyone else.

Concerning this calling the Apostle affirms that it is:

2. According to the purpose of God
We shall have occasion to consider it at large hereafter. At present it may appear if we consider how entirely our calling depends upon three things which are wholly dependent on the purpose of God and as much out of the power of man as the wind and rain can be.

(i) The death of Christ
Unless God in his great love had given his Son to die for our sins, none could have been called, but all mankind must have sunk forever under the weight of his wrathful indignation denounced against sin.

(ii) The knowledge of the gospel (Rom. 10.14,15). And this surely is not affected but by the purpose of God. It must be resolved into his will:

(a) That the gospel is known in this land, while many parts of the globe are without it.

(b) That you were born in this land rather than in the East Indies, or in Africa.

(c) That you should be born or brought into the place where the gospel is preached, for alas it is far from being known everywhere amongst us (Amos 4.7).

(iii) The application of it to your hearts
It is said, The Lord opened the heart of Lydia, surely not without having purposed so to do, and if he had not done the same for you, you had rejected and despised it to this day. I am sure if you are a true believer, you will willingly give God all the glory of your conversion.

The common objection against this, that then there is no necessity of diligence on our parts in the use of means, I hope to show you in time is so far from being just, that the very contrary is true. And that nothing can make it reasonable to attend to them if their success is not ensured by the purpose of God.

The uses of this point are many:

1. To believers it teaches:

1.1 Humility
(1 Cor. 4.7): This tends to lay the creature low, and to check our aspiring thoughts as if we were better than other[s].

1.2 Forbearance
We are apt to be angry with poor sinners, but this will lead us to pity, pray and hope.

1.3 Comfort
If you are indeed called, you may conclude upon this ground that you shall be saved to the uttermost. And do you not need such an assurance, when you feel how weak you are and consider how many are rising up against you?

2. To sinners

It affords encouragement to turn from their sins and seek the Lord. The Lord has spared you thus long, has brought his salvation again to your ears. Do you find yourselves inclined to hear his voice? Take courage – it is his purpose to save such sinners as you in this way. He has saved many – why not you? O wait upon him and he will.

CHAPTER TWELVE

verse 29 (1)

*For whom he did foreknow, he also did predestinate to be
conformed to the image of his Son, that he might be
the firstborn among many brethren.*

The various senses which different persons affix to the same
words of scripture, and the great variety of opinions which are
to be found amongst those who profess to derive all their opinions from the book of God, and especially the exceeding posi-
tiveness with which each party maintains their own side, are
very discouraging and perplexing to enquiring minds. Satan
often makes a handle of these things and suggests: You see
they cannot agree among themselves – join with which sort
you will you may probably be wrong at last – as good therefore let them dispute it out and give yourself no trouble about
it. But this is a cheat he would put upon us. Supposing the
word of God is true and that it has a meaning, the more uncertainty we observe in others about that meaning, so much the
more diligence we should use to understand it for ourselves.
The more positive we find people and the more we observe of
the ill effects of their heart, so much the more should we distrust our own spirits, be afraid of seeing with other people's
eyes and seek the direction of the Spirit of God which is promised to guide us into all necessary truth.

It is plain that the people of God differ in their sentiments
on some points, yet it will not therefore follow that they go all
upon uncertainties, for there are some things, such as the evil
of sin, the excellency of Jesus, and the beauty of holiness, in
which they are all agreed to a man. That they differ in others
is owing partly to the different degrees of light from the Spirit

of God, partly to the undue regard they pay to their favourite teachers, partly to the difference among them in point of diligence, spirituality and application to the Lord by humble prayer and studying his word, partly to the time of their standing, for they are not taught everything at once, but by degrees (Prov. 4.18), as they are able to bear it.

It is however a desirable thing to have the judgment clearly established in every point of the revealed will of God, and to avoid the inconveniencies on the right hand and on the left in matters of controversy. The way to this is not by noisy disputation but by consulting the word and waiting upon God. If you had received a letter of very great consequence to your peace and there was something in it which you did not well understand, suppose you showed it to several of your neighbours and each one gave you a different sense of the words, this would but increase your perplexity. But if you carried it to the person that wrote it, he could clear up your doubts at once. This is what you should do in scripture difficulties (1 Cor. 2.11).

But as prayer should be joined with enquiry and means on our part, when you are desirous to know which opinion is right or more probable, I would offer you these rules:

1. Be not determined by one or two texts but see which is most agreeable to the general strain of the scripture.

2. Take experience along with you, for this, though not to be depended on in the first place, is a good help to understand the scripture – see which sense is most agreeable to what passes within you and around you and which best answers to the dealings of God with yourself and others.

3. When you have thus come to the best view of the case you can obtain, do not think you must be necessarily wrong because there are perhaps some objections which you are not able fully to answer, but consider if there are not as strong or stronger objections against the other side. We are poor weak creatures – the clearing of every difficulty is not what we are called to, but to seek that kind of light which may strengthen and feed our souls. Therefore:

4. Compare the tendency of different opinions: this is an excellent rule, if we can but apply it fairly – whatever is of God, has a sure tendency to ascribe glory to him, to exclude boasting from the creature, to promote the love and practice of holiness and increase our dependence upon his grace and faithfulness, that we may not be weary and faint in our minds.

You see I enter upon the subject of my text with much caution. I am going to speak upon high points and I would not darken counsel by words without knowledge. And I recommend the same caution to you. Take nothing upon trust, but examine for yourselves. Only pray for a simple, humble spirit and entreat the Lord either to confirm you if you are right, or to teach you better when you are mistaken. *Above all be afraid* of having only the notion of truth in your heads without the savour of it in your hearts.

In this verse the Apostle speaks:

Of two sovereign acts of God, respecting fallen man:

1. Foreknowledge. *Whom he did foreknow.*
2. Predestination. *Them also he did [predestinate].*

Of two great ends he had in view:

3. The one immediately respecting his creatures, that they should *be conformed to the image of his Son.*

4. The other respecting the glory of Christ. *That he might be the first born among many brethren.* Or in all things have the pre-eminence.

Each of these four points, will probably demand a distinct discourse to illustrate.

1. Foreknowledge

That this belongeth to God is generally allowed. But the Apostle does not intend here his universal foreknowledge, whereby all creatures and events are ever present to his view, but a particular foreknowledge which implies favour and approbation. This is plain because there is a chain in every clause of this and the next verse – whom he foreknew – he also – called, justified, glorified.

With respect to this there is a twofold judgment.

1.1 Some would understand it, that with respect to the way of redemption, that it should be through faith in Jesus and obedience to the truth this was of God's appointment; but with respect to the persons, it only means that God foreknew who would receive the Gospel and bid it welcome and has surely ordained and predestinated that all such shall be justified and glorified.

1.2 Others suppose that the just and holy God considering all mankind as dead in sin and dead in law, all equally liable to condemnation, he might with the highest justice have left them every one to perish. But in his great love he provided a Saviour and made choice according to his own infinite wisdom of the very persons to whom he would afford that grace and light of his Spirit, without which they would have despised Christ and rejected the counsel of God against themselves, as well as others. So that the main and first reason why some believe in Christ and account him their all in all, while others see nothing desirable in him, is owing to this foreknowledge and predestination of God. This latter I think is clearly taught in scripture and accounts for all the appearances which usually take place when the gospel is known. But because human nature is prone to run into extremes, and many who hold this side of the question have said harsh and hasty things which I do not undertake to defend, I would promise before I proceed to the proof of it:

(i) That when I ascribe the salvation of any sinner, wholly to the Sovereign pleasure and appointment of God, I do not mean that the Lord acts without a reason, but only that he has not made us acquainted with his reasons, and therefore it is most safe and modest for us to resolve all into his good pleasure. Without doubt the Lord does not choose at random as we might take a handful of corn out of a bushel. He has a reason why he sends his gospel to one nation rather than another, why he affords his grace to Peter and withholds it from Judas – but these reasons, though perfectly consistent with his wisdom, holiness and equity, are within himself and not yet made known to us. Perhaps at the great day he may afford farther light into the ground of his determinations than he has plainly made known to us in his word. Then his ways shall be justified and every mouth stopped.

(ii) That whatever the reasons may be, any goodness or distinction in the creature cannot be the cause. The Lord did not foreknow or appoint any to salvation because he foresaw that they were or would be better than others in themselves but in order to make them so.

Let us now examine this doctrine by the rules I mentioned at the beginning.

1. It is not only supported by several striking single texts such as Romans 9.16,18, John 1.13 and 6.44, with many others, but it agrees with the current strain of scripture, which represent all mankind:

1.1 As dead in trespasses and sins, utterly incapable of performing one spiritual act and under the rule of Satan (Eph. 2.2).

1.2 As being alienated from God and at enmity with him by wicked works (Col. 1.21).

1.3 As having a peculiar aversion and dislike to God's appointed means of salvation (1 Cor. 1.23).

2. This doctrine answers to experience and observation. Consider:

2.1 With regard to others
   (i) If the knowledge of Christ is necessary to salvation. How else shall we account for the dispensation of the gospel being offered to so few of the children of men? (Acts 4.12). This is so plain to those who deny the sovereignty of grace that they almost make the gospel of little or no value in endeavouring to prove that many may be saved who never heard of it. But then besides the dishonourable imputation it casts on the wisdom of God, what shall we do with Romans 10.13,14? But of this more hereafter.

   (ii) Who received the gospel at first. Was the thief upon the Cross, or persecuting Saul, or the Corinthians spoken of (1 Cor. 6.11), in a better state than their neighbours? If you enquire into the cause of St Paul's success at Corinth the Lord himself assigns it (Acts 18.10).

(iii) How comes it that those who in the judgment of men have been the best prepared, who are deemed the wise and prudent, the sober and well behaved, have generally rejected? The fewest of these and with the greatest apparent difficulty have been brought to believe in Jesus.

2.2 With regard to yourselves

I believe if the argument is confined here, and you do not think yourself concerned to vindicate God's dealings with others – all who have known his grace will be of one mind – will you say that it was in consequence of some good in you, that the Lord rewarded you with faith? No, if you know your own hearts, you will say, To us belongeth nothing but shame and confusion of face.

I should proceed to consider on which side the strongest objections lie, but this must be deferred. In the meantime:

1. No particular person has any ground from the word of God to think himself excluded. The invitation is to all who desire. Have you the desire? If it is of that sort that stirs you up to wait closely upon God it shall be satisfied. This is good news for great sinners, that it depends not on works but on the free purpose of God. If it was otherwise, what hope could there be for those who see themselves as they are?

2. Believers rejoice – praise the love that thought of you before you had a being (Jer. 31.3). This love shall not be disappointed. He that has begun the good work will accomplish it.

CHAPTER THIRTEEN

verse 29 (2)

*For whom he did foreknow, he also did predestinate to be
conformed to the image of his Son, that he might be
the firstborn among many brethren.*

If the doctrine I am upon is agreeable to the general strain of
scripture and answers to experience and observation we have
a sufficient warrant to adhere to it, though we should not be
able to satisfy ourselves or others clearly with respect to every
objection that may be started. While there is so much darkness, unbelief, pride, prejudice and impurity in our hearts we
must not expect a full and comprehensive view of divine truths.
We must believe nothing if we wait till every scruple and difficulty is settled. If there are objections against our sentiments,
there are objections against the other likewise. I proceed therefore to examine according to the rule proposed:

3. Against which side the strongest objections lie
Those who think we carry the notion of God's sovereign appointment in the salvation of sinners too high give such reasons as these for their dissent from us:

3.1 When they consider how few receive the gospel, in comparison with the millions who never heard of it and the multitudes who reject and dishonour it, are afraid it bears hard upon
the goodness and mercy of God to suffer such unknown num-
bers to perish – and to avoid this they suppose that the Almighty is willing and desirous that every one of them should
be saved and has provided sufficient means for that purpose.
But we may observe in answer:

(i) That this objection and supposition seems to spring from too slight a sense of the evil of sin and the justice and holiness of God. The Lord does not condemn any strictly speaking for not having that faith which is his peculiar gift, but they are condemned already by the holy law. In this case he might have left all mankind to perish. If he had saved but one single soul it would have been an act of undeserved mercy and none could have had right to complain. Those who never heard of the gospel will not be judged by it but by that law, the traces of which sufficiently strong to condemn them are written in their hearts (Rom 2.10 [Rom 2.15?]). And those who reject the gospel do only thereby discover the evil which was in their heart before they heard of it and confirm the righteous judgment of God in wilfully refusing his appointed means of salvation.

(ii) The objection does not at all remove the difficulty upon their own principles. Since after all in fact, the greatest number of those who have the means of grace afforded them perish at last, so that if God did certainly *will* their salvation he is disappointed, which is a supposition highly unworthy of us to make.

3.2 They oppose[10] a few texts which in the sound of the words seem at first to favour their cause, such as Ezekiel 18.32, Luke 13.34, 1 Timothy 2.4 and the like. But:

(i) I have observed already that we are not to think our sense supported by a few detached texts only – the general strain of the scripture is (as I have shown) on the other side. And we can produce single texts as strong for us (Rom. 9.18; John 6.44; Matt. 11.23 and 13.11). But the scripture cannot be at variance with itself. Many things are occasionally spoken after the manner of men as where God is said to repent, grieve and the like. There certainly is a consistent sense in his word and if we cannot always reconcile and make it out, let the difficulty be charged upon the weakness of our understandings.

(ii) We answer as before – either a lower sense must be given to these expressions than they allow, or else we must say the will of God is disappointed and overpowered by the will of his creatures, which cannot be.

3.3 It is objected that to fix the salvation of particular persons wholly in the foreappointment of God is entirely to set aside the reasonableness of the use of means. I answer:

(i) If the means are considered as instruments put into men's hands wherewith to work out their own salvation, we confess it. Neither prayer, reading, hearing or resolving, considered as the creature's act, can bring one spark of spiritual life into the soul. And for this we may appeal to the experience of many, perhaps some of you. The form of godliness alone is as distant and different from the power, as a picture or statue is from a living man. But:

(ii) Consider the means as of God's appointment and which he has promised to bless. Then the consideration that he has foreappointed them as the method by which he will bring us to the knowledge of himself should bind us the more strongly to the use of them. Nay,

(iii) The only consideration that can make it rational to use them at all is this very appointment and assurance that they shall not be in vain. As I show hereafter.

3.4 Some oppose this doctrine from a fear that it encourages licentiousness. If this could be proved, undoubtedly we ought to renounce it upon the spot. For every doctrine that is from God must be according to godliness, and I hope in my next, when I consider the tendency of the point we are upon, to show you that this charge is utterly false. At present:

(i) We acknowledge that some who favour this doctrine, and hold it as a notion in their heads do walk unworthy of the gospel. But the question is, whether this is owing to the doctrine they profess to hold, or to their abuse of it. When St Paul had stated the foundation truth of the gospel, justification by the blood of Christ, he knew there would be those, as there are too many in our day, who would turn this grace of God into lasciviousness and say, Let us continue in sin that grace may abound. But does he upon this account retract what he said? No. He contents himself with expressing his abhorrence of such a thought, for he knew that no heart that had indeed tasted that the Lord is gracious could listen to such a wild and abominable inference. The same reasoning will hold here – we must give up every precious gospel truth, if we will not contend for them till wicked men cease to pervert the right ways of the Lord. If therefore some are found who presume to say, If the Lord has chosen me, he will call me in his own time and in the meanwhile I will go contentedly on in my sins, it proves only this – that man is as so desperately wicked by nature, that he can resolve and dare to be wicked, because God is good.

(ii) May we not as well charge the other as tending to licentiousness! For, setting aside a few who have been brought up under the preaching of free grace and got a little knowledge in their heads – and all the openly profane and wicked in every place will profess to hold something of a power in man to help forward his own salvation – take a survey of those who oppose predestination and we shall find serious people who believe in Jesus Christ for life and according to his gospel are much not the smallest number. And we cannot think it gives any weight to their sentiments that we see in general not only the self righteous but those who live in sin, swearers, drunkards, liars etc., agree with them thus far. Our brethren who differ from us would be angry if we should charge the gross outward wickedness in which the world is buried, as a consequence of their rejecting predestination.

These I think are the chief objections raised against the doctrine of God's sovereignty. Let us now object[11] in our turn and consider the difficulties to which their scheme is liable.

1. We may object the verses before us, those I lately mentioned and many others which assert this doctrine as expressly as words can do. And not to rest the cause upon a few texts, we object the whole body of the scripture and the manner of God's dealing with the children of men from the earliest ages. Abraham was an idolater till God called him. The Lord's word to Jeremiah is express: chapter 1.5. St Paul speaks in the same manner of himself: Galatians 1.15. And the reason why any are brought to know and love the Lord is universally given: Jeremiah 31.3. So our Lord to his apostles: John 15.16. And in the prayer before his passion he makes a notable distinction between those whom the Father had given him, and the men of the world. Of these latter he says, I pray not for them.

2. We may oppose – the manner in which God actually calls his people. Lydia was one among many hearers. Why did she believe? We are told why – the Lord opened her heart. The jailer in the same chapter had given sufficient proof just before his conversion how little he was prepared for it in himself.

Saul was breathing out threatenings and slaughter till the
moment when Jesus spoke to him. He had several companions,
not one perhaps so furious as himself. We read not that they,
though struck to the ground likewise, were savingly changed.
Why was he singled out from the rest? The Lord tells us, He
is a chosen vessel to me. And we see it so to this day – it has
often happened that two companions in wickedness have gone
to the same preaching with the same views to ridicule what
they should hear. One of them has returned profane as he went,
while the other was pierced. Both heard the same words. Both
went in the same disposition. To what then can the different
effect be ascribed but to the power and grace of God? And
does not this imply choice and consequently foreknowledge?
For the Lord to whom past, present and to come are the same,
does not take up new designs today which he thought not of
yesterday, as we do.

3. We object. That those who deny this appointment of God
and ascribe the conversion of sinners to anything else in whole
or in part but his good pleasure, do in effect deny that man is
totally dead in trespasses and sins and suppose that he has
some power in himself to turn to God before the Holy Spirit
works upon his heart. Now where can this something be? Not
in the understanding, for that is stark blind; not in the will for
that by nature is stubborn and obstinate as the wild ass's colt,
not in the affections for these are enslaved and buried in the
love of sin and the world. If it is said that some persons are of
a more sober and thoughtful turn, let it be observed that the
most of these are generally the warmest opposers of the gospel
of Christ that we meet with. Publicans and harlots enter into
the kingdom before them.

4. We farther say that unless we allow this foreknowledge and
predestination we must suppose it highly precarious and un-

certain whether any one of the children of men should ever believe in Christ. The greatest part do reject him and why not all, since all are by nature alike? Had it depended upon the will of man, Jesus might have lived and died in vain, without a single disciple. A difference there plainly is. The Apostle asks, Who made thee to differ? Now who that knows anything of himself will dare to say, I made myself to differ? It is well therefore that one clause of the covenant of grace established with and in Christ is: Thy people shall be willing in the day of thy power (Ps. 110.3). We must therefore either give the glory to God or take it to ourselves.

(1) Do you assent to the doctrine of sovereign grace? Take heed that you do not abuse it. Many contend for the foundation who are not built upon it. Give all diligence to make your election sure by your calling.

(2) Do any still differ with me? But do you love the Lord Jesus and walk in his ways? Go on – look to him. Whereunto we have attained let us walk by the same rule. If in anything you are otherwise minded he can reveal even this unto you.

(3) To some I know these truths are precious and comfortable. You may sing, Salvation hath God appointed for walls and bulwarks. The foundation of God standeth sure. The Lord knoweth them that are his, and let every one that nameth the name of Christ depart from iniquity.

CHAPTER FOURTEEN

verse 29 (3)

For whom he did foreknow, he also did predestinate to be conformed to the image of his Son, that he might be the firstborn among many brethren.

Though the doctrine of God's sovereign foreknowledge is clearly revealed in scripture and affords much consolation to those who spiritually understand it, yet it is not of that kind which is absolutely and essentially necessary to be received. A person may be a child of God and under his gracious operations, who cannot as yet embrace it. It is opposed by many plausible objections. For this reason I do not very frequently insist upon subjects of this sort, but as it necessarily lay before me in these verses I thought it a fit opportunity for once to handle this and the points immediately connected with it something at large – and I shall be therefore detained a considerable time upon this and the following verse. I have not yet finished my first general head. But thus far we have proceeded – I have endeavoured to show that it is agreeable to scripture and experience and I have stated and compared the principle objections against it, with those which may be urged against the contrary sentiment.

I shall now:

(4) Examine into the tendency of this doctrine, which is a rule (if rightly managed) very useful to determine points of controversy. But there is some skill and experience necessary in applying it. For on which side soever the truth is supposed to lie there will be loose and disorderly retainers[12] enough, to bring their profession into discredit. On the other hand, the

Spirit of the Lord is not bound, will not be bound, within the limits of a name and party. He has a spiritual people on both sides [of] the question. We do not therefore mean to compare with others or to intimate that we are better than they. If any who differ from us are enabled to walk humbly and holily before God, we desire to rejoice in it and to pray for their farther increase. And if (as we cannot but think) [it] is the[13] case that we have the advantage of them in points of clearness, we have reason to be so much the more humbled that any who have received fewer talents should outstrip us in their returns of obedience and love. When the question is concerning the improvement we make of the many helps our gracious God has afforded us, the most becoming answer that we can make is to shrink into the dust before him and cry out, Unclean, Unclean. We do not therefore desire to exult ourselves or to pull down any. Nor shall I make any comparison but only in order to remove the charge thrown against this doctrine as encouraging licentiousness. I shall endeavour to show that (however poorly we improve it) it has a proper tendency and suitableness to promote the great ends and designs for which God has revealed his word unto us.

There is a touchstone to this purpose proposed by an old author (and recommended by the late Mr Hervey[14]). As I can offer you nothing more suitable, I shall make use of this. The general designs of God, by the methods of salvation which he has appointed, are:

1. to humble the sinner
2. to exalt the Saviour
3. to produce holiness in heart and life

Let us embrace or reject the point in hand according as it shall be found to bear this trial.

4.1 Surely it tends to humble the sinner and to fall in with the Lord's professed design (Isa. 23.9) to stain the pride of all human glory. This and this alone stops every mouth as to boasting and leaves the soul nothing to glory in but the Lord. How prone are men by nature to set a value upon something as:

(i) Outward privileges (Matt. 3.9).

(ii) Natural or acquired qualifications (Jer. 9.23; 1 Cor. 1.19; 26, 27).

(iii) Moral characters (Matt. 21.31).

(iv) Diligent endeavours. As though the Lord was indebted to them for the great pains they take like those: Isaiah 58.3. But what says the word? Romans 9.18.

(v) Gifts and labours (the especial temptation of favoured ministers), but Zechariah 4.6. They find it as Luke 10.6. If the Lord has any to call, they speak to good purpose. If not, in vain they rise early and take rest. They may have the comfort of the word returning to themselves, but they can do no good to others.

But when the soul is thus stripped of everything, sees a foundation of hope, and begins to taste that the Lord is gracious, how does a view of foreknowledge and sovereignty humble. Then all these texts so mortifying to human pride are assented to and the repeated enquiry and wonder is, Why me, Lord, Why me?

> Why was I made to hear thy voice
> And enter while there's room?
> When thousands make a wretched choice
> And rather starve than come?
> 'Twas the same love that made the feast
> That sweetly forced us in;
> Else we had still refused to taste
> And perished in our sin.

4.2 Whatever humbles the sinner, exalts the Saviour of course – this is a sure consequence. The more we sink in our own esteem, the more excellent and glorious will Jesus appear. Why do so many see no form or comeliness in him? Because they are so well satisfied in themselves. The whole may give the physician a good word, but the sick alone know how to prize him. And here I can but remark a difference between those who have nothing to trust to but free grace, and such as ascribe a little, at least, to some good disposition in man. We assent to and admire many things that they say are the subject of sanctification. We acknowledge its importance, its excellence, its beauty. But we could wish they join more with us in exalting the Redeemer's name. Their experience seems to lead to talk of themselves, of the change that is wrought, and the much that depends upon their own watchfulness and striving. We likewise are thankful if we can see any change – we desire to be found watching likewise – but when our hopes are most alive, it is less from a view of the imperfect beginnings of grace in our hearts, than from an apprehension of *him* who is our *all in all*. His person, his love, his sufferings, his intercession, compassion, fullness and faithfulness – these are our delightful themes, which leave us little leisure (when in our best frame) to speak of ourselves. How does the heart soften and the eyes melt when we can get a little liberty to speak of him. For we had no help in time past, nor can have in time to come, but from him alone. If any have contributed a mite to their own salvation, it was more than we could do – if any were obedient to his first call, it was not our case – if any were prepared to receive him beforehand, we know that we were at the greatest distance. We needed sovereign, irresistible grace or we had been lost forever. If any feel a power of their own to help them, we must confess ourselves poorer than they. We cannot watch except he watches with us. We cannot strive except he strives in us. We cannot stand one moment except he holds us up. And we believe we must surely perish after all, except his faithfulness is engaged to keep us. It only remains to be considered if this way of thinking will afford liberty or encouragement to sin or trifle, or whether:

4.3 It produces and promotes the practice of holiness. The answer will appear if we consider what are the principles which the scripture mentions as conducive to holiness. Such as:

(i) A sense of our own insufficiency. Many miscarry because they trust in themselves (Luke 14.28).

(ii) Love to Jesus (2 Cor. 5.14). Now those, if any, should love who think they owed the more and had the least to pay (Luke 7.47).

(iii) Dependence (2 Cor. 12.9).

(iv) A persuasion that our labour shall not be in vain.

All these considerations are strengthened upon the supposition that the grace of God is sovereign.

But I could wish my friends, that arguments were needless on this head and that we who have professed to hold the doctrines of free grace might more evidently vindicate and prove them in our lives. O that we were more concerned in the way to stand up for these precious truths. For after all, this is the best, if not the only way, to convince and silence gainsayers.

But does not this scheme encourage sinners to continue in their sins?

1. This objection is sometimes quite beside the purpose. We contend that no doctrines or means can change the heart with-

out efficacious almighty grace comes in. Therefore if it is found so in truth, it should not be charged *against* our doctrine, but rather admitted as a proof of it.

2. The call to believe and repent is universal and we are encouraged to publish it because we know the Lord will make it effectual.

> Therefore thus saith the Lord, Turn ye from your evil ways, for why will you die?

You cannot be excused, except you have and do use the power God has already given you.

3. Those who abuse this branch of gospel doctrine abuse every other.

4. To tell people that they have a power within themselves to turn to God when they please, is quite as likely to harden them in their sins and put off all enquiries. Yet:

5. It is undoubtedly so abused by many. But wo to those by whom the offence cometh – who cause the ways of truth to be evil spoken. See their character and doom: Matthew 25.24-30.

CHAPTER FIFTEEN

verse 29 (4)

For whom he did foreknow, he also did predestinate
to be conformed to the image of his Son, that he
might be the firstborn among many brethren.

I have finished what I proposed from the first general head in this verse and proceed to the second, predestination.

2. Them also he predestinated

Foreknowledge, of which we have spoken at large, is considered chiefly with respect to the persons. Predestination refers to:

1. The *end* which the Lord has in view in their behalf and of which we are to speak more at large from the next clause.

2. The *means* by which he has determined to accomplish this end.

The sum of both is – that the Lord has a people known to himself long before they knew him – that he has appointed these to salvation, to holiness and happiness, and that he directs all his dispensations towards them so as to be subservient to these great ends and so as best to display the exceeding riches of his glorious grace in their behalf.

Let us by way of illustration consider this *predestination* of God as designing and accomplishing a temporal covenant, the settlement of Israel in Canaan, and then apply the leading turns of their history to his dealings with the spiritual Israel.

The objects of this foreknowledge in that case were the

children of Abraham according to the flesh – but not all these, but those only who descended from Isaac by Jacob his younger son. The seed of Ishmael and Esau were excluded – not because they were more unfit or more unworthy in themselves, but because he so appointed, who has a right to do what he will with his own. Now concerning Jacob's posterity he revealed his purpose long before Jacob himself was born, that they should certainly in the end possess the land, but that in their way to it they should be detained long in Egypt, led through the wilderness, suffer many hardships, be opposed by many enemies, but that none of these things should prevent his promises from being fulfilled. Now none of these things were necessary till his appointment made them so. He might have chosen another people, have led them by another way. He could easily have inclined Pharaoh to dismiss them at the first word or made all their enemies friends. But the method he chose was evidently suited to manifest his own power and to show that his choice of them and all his goodness towards them was undeserved and free.

The Lord conducts himself in a like way of free grace and marvellous power towards his children of the new covenant whom he has foreknown, even all those who at the great day shall be found at the right hand of the judgment seat. In themselves they were no better than those on the left hand. The difference is that it pleased the Lord to make them his people. But this first difference between them and others has made them to differ throughout. By nature they were all in worse than Egyptian bondage and his predestination respects the means of their deliverance, the methods of their support and their final victory over all enemies and opposition. He does not begin with them when they first begin to seek after him, but he thought of them before they had a being. They could not possibly choose at what time or in what country they would appear in the world but he chose for them. And as they grow up in life, while they have often one view, he has another – their evil hearts often lead them to plunge themselves deeper and deeper in sin, but his restraining grace keeps them from doing all they would and his providence preserves them when they seem bent upon ruining themselves. He permits a variety of cases among them but none is found too hard for his power and this variety displays his manifold wisdom and infallible skill and the exact truth of his holy word. Everything tends to illustrate the dreadful nature of sin, the powerful efficacy of grace and the value and necessity of a Saviour and the certainty of the promises.

2.1 The end
The predestination of God has appointed:

(i) The knowledge of Christ as the great means of salvation. There is no other name given – and this is all sufficient.

(ii) That the interest in this Redeemer should be by faith, to the utter exclusion of all works of every kind (Rom. 4.16).

(iii) That faith should be ordinarily wrought by the preached gospel – or at least by the word. In consequence of this, when the Lord has many people to call at one time or place, he usually sends his gospel means to them. If he has a few scattered here and there, his providence or Spirit usually leads them in the way of means and ministers, or provides them some help which by his blessing is made effectual to his purposed end.

(iv) That they should generally be an afflicted people, that his power may be displayed in their behalf (Acts 14.22). Hence they are mostly poor, tempted, despised – they are led through a wilderness, through fire, through water, but at length they shall be brought out.

(v) That they should be a holy people. That they should not have the name of his children without the temper and disposition of a child. And therefore he is not ashamed to be called their God.

2.2 The means
This predestination on God's part points out the path of duty on ours.

(i) The use of means
The stale objection, if God has chosen me I may be careless, is vain and foolish. If God has chosen you, or before you can know it to your comfort, you will highly prize those means by which he has promised to work.

(ii) To prize the truth
There is but one doctrine – that of a crucified Saviour which God had promised to bless. Take heed therefore how – and what you hear.

(iii) To renounce self righteousness
For God has determined and declared that he will not accept it.

(iv) To welcome the cross – for it leads to a crown
Think not you are in a state of favour because you see no sorrow. Think not that you cannot be a child, because your afflictions are great (Heb. 12.4).

(v) To examine the bent of our hearts and lives
You have no right to the blessings if sin is not your burthen and holiness your great desire.

CHAPTER SIXTEEN

verse 29 (5)

*For whom he did foreknow, he also did predestinate to be
conformed to the image of his Son, that he might be
the firstborn among many brethren.*

The subjects we have been considering of late from this verse
are rejected by many as points of curious speculation at the
best, if they have not a dangerous tendency to weaken the
obligations to morality, where too many others who profess
to hold and admire them, who contend for them in words,
bring them into discredit by their lives and conduct. I have
been (of late taken up with) endeavouring to answer objections and guard against offences, which though sometimes
necessary, does not afford that nourishment of food to the
young and the weak in the faith which they are waiting for. I
am glad therefore to proceed according to my purposed method
to speak of the great ends for which the Lord has chosen and
appointed his people - the text speaks of two and the first of
these is the third general head which I designed to consider.

3. To be conformed to the image of his Son (see Vol. 4 page
59)[16]

This is the great end of predestination – that those whom
he foreknew, should not remain in the darkness and misery of
their natural estate, but that, having the eyes of their understanding opened to behold the beauty of holiness in Jesus, they
should be changed into the same image. Two things offer themselves from the words, which I shall briefly notice as I pass
along.

1. It is supposed that the Lord's people are by nature destitute of this glorious image even as others. See how St Paul describes himself and brethren before conversion (Titus 3.3).

2. That Christ is the standard or pattern of that true goodness which we should seek after – and that no person or action is good, but so far as it is conformable to the mind that was in Christ Jesus. This rule will sooner or later stop the mouths of all boasters of their own righteousness. Many a fair outside which men agree to flatter with the names of morality and virtue, will be cast out by the great Judge because not conformable to the mind that was in Christ. We must act from the same principles, walk by the same rule, and have the same ends in view which he had, or all our goodness is nothing worth.

The conformity to the image of the Son of God which all his people are appointed unto is threefold –

3.1 In grace (John 1.16)
The fullness is in him and they receive grace for grace, feature for feature – the first impressions are indeed faint, but they grow into a stronger resemblance as they grow in his knowledge. We do not here consider the whole of Christ's conduct because in many things he acted as Mediator, but in his ordinary carriage as a Man amongst men the beauty of holiness shone forth and his people copy after him. The chief branches of this image are:

(i) Spirituality
He was dead to the world and devoted to God. His heart and conversation were in heaven and it was his meat and drink to do his father's will.

(ii) Compassion
Going about doing good. Not only relieving all who came to him but sharing their sorrows and sympathising with them (Luke 7.13; John 11.35).

(iii) Meekness
Matthew 11.29: He had no desire of applause, no resentment of injuries, but was gentle, forebearing and forgiving under the worst treatment (1 Pet. 2.23; John 18.23).

(iv) Constancy
Maintaining his profession to the end, unmoved by all the temptations of Satan and all the malice of men.

Such was Jesus. Those are most happy who are most like him, but alas we may all take up a complaint. However in each of these respects, all who are called by grace have a begun likeness.

3.2 In affliction
As he was, so are they in the world and for the like reasons (John 15.19; 1 John 3.1). It is a fixed law that through much tribulation we must enter the kingdom. The members must be like the head and this puts a great honour upon a believer's afflictions – they are the afflictions of Christ. The greatest he sustained in his own body, but he has left a little for his people to fill up, that they may have fellowship with him and he with them (Col. 1.24; 2 Cor. 1.5). If any of his children could pass without affliction and tasting of his cup they would lose a considerable honour. Therefore they are despised by men, tempted by Satan, tried by God, that they may be like their Lord, may tread in his footsteps and may pass through sufferings to a kingdom, as he did.

But since affliction is the lot of all, how may we know if

our sufferings are of that sort which prove a conformity to Christ?

(i) Whatever we suffer conscientiously for his sake and the truth.

(ii) Whatever we suffer in the spirit and temper of Christ – when we submit to the will of God and are patient towards the instruments by which he is pleased to afflict us.

3.3 In glory
To those who are thus conformed here, there remains hereafter a conformity in glory. So sure as we suffer with him we shall reign with them. This conformity will be complete and perpetual:

(i) In our souls
When we see him as he is, we shall be perfectly like him (1 John 3.2).

(ii) In our bodies
They shall be made like to his glorious body (Phil. 3.21). Then shall the righteous shine forth like the sun.

This subject may be applied to:

1. Conviction
See the folly and wickedness of those who despise and hate the people of God – hate them for their spirituality – despise them for their afflictions. What is the ground of the quarrel? Only that they have some little likeness to God's dear Son and the smallest degree of this is more than the world can well bear with patience. O the enmity of the carnal mind. But remember who has said, He that despiseth you, despiseth me.

Whosoever offendeth or despiseth one of these little ones that
believe in me etc..

2. Trial

Do you make a profession? Examine the truth of your grace
by the fruits: are you in any manner conformed to Jesus? If
you hope you are, examine concerning your growth. Does your
conformity increase?

3. Comfort

What, are you afflicted and does the Lord sanctify your troubles and enable you to bear them in some degree of the Spirit
of Christ? Then take courage – such afflictions are a proof of
sonship, a token for good, and they shall be soon ended. The
time is short. Ere long your conformity in glory will come on.
Live upon the prospect, endeavour to keep the thought always
near your heart. It will be an excellent cordial under every
trouble.

CHAPTER SEVENTEEN

verse 29 (6)

*For whom he did foreknow, he also did predestinate to be
conformed to the image of his Son, that he might be
the firstborn among many brethren.*

The Lord's gracious design in the salvation of his people has
respect to a still farther and higher end, the manifestation of
his own glory in the person of Christ. This remains to be spoken to from the verse.

4. That he might be the firstborn among many brethren
This expression is taken from the Old Testament usage. The
firstborn was considered as the head of the family. The rest
depended on him. He had a double blessing, an eminence –
both in dignity and possession. The sense therefore is the same
with Colossians 1.18. It is not spoken of Christ with regard to
his divine nature, singly, but as he is God man, the Mediator
between God and man, the Head and Saviour of his body the
Church, the temple of his human nature inhabited by all the
fullness of the Godhead. While he was upon earth he was of
no repute. He was left to hang dead and naked upon the cross.
He was put in the grave like another man. But the grave could
not keep him – he arose, he ascended, he entered into glory
and from thence he sends down his awakening, sanctifying,
governing Spirit, by which he brings his people to conformity
with himself and will shortly bring them home to his kingdom. Then they shall shine forth like sons. They will so perfectly resemble him that he will not be ashamed to call them
brethren. They shall be acknowledged as such by the Lord, by
his angels and even by their enemies. On the other hand, the

work will then appear entirely his own and he shall have the praise. They will cast their crowns at his feet and say, Thou, Thou only, art worthy. Theirs shall be the comfort, that he is not ashamed to call them brethren, and he shall have the glory of the firstborn. Observe:

4.1 The Lord Jesus is *the firstborn*
The honour and glory of the work of redemption belong to him.

(i) It is the Father's will (John 5.23; Phil. 2.9,10,11).

(ii) He challenges it to himself (Isa 45.23,24; Rev. 1.18).

(iii) It is paid him in heaven by his redeemed people and by the angels (Rev. 5).

(iv) It is paid him by his called people on earth. And this proves that he has given them a meetness for the inheritance of the saints in light. They gladly say, All my *springs* (Ps. 87.7).

(a) They adore his person. They contemplate him as the brightness of the Father's glory – as possessed of all power, authority and wisdom. Here there is a depth – unsearchable riches of glory, of which we see but little at present, but that little puts out the light of all created beauty and glory. See Psalm 45.

(b) They admire his love. This consideration is heightened by the former. The clearer views we have who he is, the more we shall be affected with the thought of what he has done. The reason why the world takes so little notice of his sufferings is because they do not know him.

(c) They depend on his grace. They feel themselves weak but they see an all sufficiency in him – able to feed, to guard, to guide and to perfect – and to him they look, renouncing thoughts of every other.

(d) They rejoice in him as their portion. *None but Christ* is their motto. They are convinced that he, and he only, can make them happy.

I know no better mark by which you may judge of your own state than this – if you have high thoughts of Jesus, in his person and offices, you are assuredly a believer. But if he is not chief in your heart, take care lest you flatter yourself with a false hope.

The people of God have a high honour:

4.2 They are brethren to the Lord Jesus

(i) They are so in nature
(a) He has taken their nature upon him (Heb. 2.14). And in this nature of man, he is now seated on his throne and reigning over heaven and earth. He is the first fruits, the head, the forerunner – they his members, friends and brethren – and he will have them where he is.

(b) He has given to them a divine nature from himself. And for this cause he is not ashamed of them, because they partake of his Spirit and walk as he walked.

(ii) In states
(a) Is he the Son, the heir of God? They through him are children and fellow heirs and God in witness thereof has sent down his Spirit into their hearts whereby they cry, Abba Father.

(b) Did he live a suffering life? So do they, they have fellowship with him in opposition, temptation, etc..

(c) Is he now in glory? There they shall likewise come – he has promised it to them (John 14.3) and demanded for them (ch. 17.24).

4.3 They are many brethren

(i) Brethren among themselves, of the same family and father, begotten of the same word, fed from the same table, led by the same Spirit and hoping for the same glory. Hence arises a strong motive to the duties they owe to each other such as love, tenderness, forbearance, assistance, etc..

(ii) Many brethren. Not many in comparison of the world, seldom many in one time or place. But when brought together at last, they will be an exceeding great multitude like the sand of the seashore innumerable.

Here then is encouragement for poor sinners. Yet there is room, the Lord's people are not yet all called. Not all (I trust) in this place – there are some men behind, for whose sakes the blessed gospel is continued amongst you. Is there not some wishing, fearing soul, that says, O that I may be one? Perhaps you are, perhaps the Lord is this moment drawing you to himself. Be not afraid, only believe. Call upon him and he will answer. Seek and you shall find. Trust him and he will be glorified in delivering you from all your fears and sins.

CHAPTER EIGHTEEN

verse 30 (1)

*Moreover whom he did predestinate, them he also called:
and whom he called, them he also justified: and whom
he justified, them he also glorified.*

This verse contains the golden chain of salvation. The first
and the last link are in heaven, the two intermediate are let
down upon earth. Those who are predestinated shall be glorified, but who they are remains a secret in the counsels of God
till his election manifests itself in due time by its effects. Whom
he has predestinated, them he also calls. Again, from the moment they are called, they enter upon a continual course of
difficulty and opposition, but having an interest in this link of
the chain, they shall surely attain to the end of it. They shall
be justified from all their sins in time and shall surely be glorified in eternity, their enemies not being able to hinder it.

At present we are to speak of the vocation and calling of
God.

1. Them he also called

It signifies that happy glorious change in state, in heart and in
life, to which all his people are brought by the power of his
grace. This has various names as it is differently considered –
with respect to the change wrought in them, it is a regeneration
or new birth from above – with respect to its certain effects it
is a conversion, a turning from sin to holiness – and with regard
to the Author and means, it is a *calling*. The vocation or calling
of God. He speaks and enables them effectually to answer and
to obey his voice.

Enquire:

1. What this calling is and how it is effected.
2. What are its fruits and evidences.

1.1 What is the calling?

(i) There is an ordinary and general calling by the preaching of the gospel; in this sense many are called, even all who come within the sound of it. This is our business as ministers, to tell you that the King has made a feast, that all things are ready, that Jesus is exalted to be a Prince and a Saviour, that there is forgiveness with him and that if you continue in your sins and prefer the present world to that life and immortality which he is brought to after, you must miserably perish. When we consider that the gospel reveals pardon, peace, honour and happiness, that in it the Lord commends the exceeding riches of his grace, addresses sinners in the most moving manner, sets before them the terror of his law to awaken their fears and the greatness of his mercy to encourage their hopes, if our hearts and experience did not teach us otherwise we should expect that all who hear would obey. But alas we find by too many proofs that this calling alone will not do.

There is therefore:

(ii) A *special* and *effectual* calling – when the word of God is accompanied with the power of his Spirit and laid so close to the heart that it will admit of no denial. This calling is not to all, but to those whom God foreknows and predestinates to eternal life, to those whom he had decreed to bring through many tribulations to glory. But if there was not such a calling secured and promised in the covenant of grace, both our preaching and your hearing would be in vain. The outward calling by the preached gospel is directed to produce this inward and this is the chief end. The Lord seldom or ever sending his messengers with his word but where he designs by the power of his grace to make that word a savour of life unto life. The gospel is not sent into every land and those countries who enjoy [it] have it not in every town. But where a town or neighbourhood enjoy the outward means, the special grace that bringeth salvation comes not into every family. One house rejoices in it while perhaps their next door neighbours account it a burden. Nay, when it enters a family it does not always reach every one in the house. Of people in the same neighbourhood, the same circumstances, the same family, one is taken and another left. Thus the word of God teaches and thus we find by experience. It is all of grace. But:

(a) This is no excuse for sinners. The Apostle who knew the heart of man tells us what answer some would make (Rom. 9.19). This is poor reasoning and will not stand before the tribunal of God. If any such are here, let me ask. Suppose you had never heard the gospel at all and had lived the same careless, unprofitable life that you do now, might not God have justly brought you into judgment for these things? If so, what advantage can you expect from living in a place where it is preached, while you neither love nor obey it? You are condemned already as a transgressor of the law and your continuing to sin, under clearer light than others have, and wilfully rejecting the only means of your recovery, does but more plainly discover the evil that is in your heart.

If you are indeed afraid of dwelling with everlasting burnings, desirous to escape from hell, the remedy is set before you: believe in Christ and you shall be saved. Can you not believe? Then pray for faith and it shall be given you. Can you not pray? If you are sincere in this confession you will never rest till you can. But alas this is not the hindrance, you are wedded to your sins and

though you may now comfort yourself in charging the
Lord foolishly he will be justified when you are condemned.

(b) Let none whose hearts are secretly stirred up to desire grace be discouraged. All the Lord's people were
as destitute of solid hope once as you can be. If there is
but a spark of light, but a faint breathing desire in your
mind, take it as a token for good and wait on the Lord
for more. You must know the calling first.

(c) Let believers praise – you know there was no difference between you and others by nature. What have you
that you have not received? Where had you been if the
Lord had not called you?

(iii) Further this calling being the Lord's own work he has:

(a) An appointed means
The great means indeed is his word either written or
preached – but I speak of means of preparation. Sometimes he has a number of people sitting in darkness together and he sends his gospel to them. Sometimes he
has one or a few that seem quite out of reach but he who
orders all things so suits his dispensations that either
willingly or against their wills they are brought under
the joyful sound. They change their habitation with quite
another view, but it is his view in permitting it – they
come out of curiosity, but he has another end in sending
them. Or perhaps he throws an acquaintance in their
way, or sends an affliction, or several afflictions like
Job's messengers one after another. For when he begins
he will make an end.

(b) An appointed time

They may lay long at the pool's side – they may be persuaded to come again and again and find no benefit, but the Lord's purpose shall take place in his own hour. Let this encourage some of you:

(1) for yourselves

Do not give up because as yet you find little done, but continue waiting. Some in our Lord's days had been long afflicted and he knew it, but he received them at last.

(2) for your friends

Some have husbands and wives and children over whom your bowels yearn – you are glad when you can see them here, you hear for them, and say this or the other thing will surely suit them. When you go home you long to find that they have been touched but still you are disappointed. Be patient, hope and pray on. You may still live to see it – or the Lord may do it after you are dead. It is not necessary for their salvation that you should know it. Commend them again and again to the Lord by prayer and you may yet meet them with joy at the great day.

I proceed by way of application, to:

1.2 The fruits and evidences of this calling

The time bids me [be] brief. Consider two characters of it from the word of God. It is:

(i) Heavenly

It comes from heaven and it leads the heart to heaven (Heb 3.1). It may be illustrated from the case of Saul who, when seek[ing] his father's asses, received the news of a kingdom which till then had never entered into his thoughts. So while we are busied with low vanities, the calling of God surprises us with a new and unthought of view, calls us from earth and leads our minds heavenward where Jesus is. This is one distinguishing mark. The men of the world seek good from the world, but those that are called, look for their good in things which the world cannot give.

(ii) Holy

2 Timothy 1.9: It gives such a view of sin as makes it hateful and burthensome, such a view of holiness as makes it more desirable than thousands of gold and silver. Besides, it engages the heart to Jesus the fountain of holiness, to the word of God the rule of holiness, to prayer for the spirit of holiness, and in this way all who are called are enabled to walk and live in a different manner to what they once did and are evidently different from the world who know not God. The Lord give us a greater increase of those evidences and teach us to hunger and thirst till we are satisfied in his kingdom.

CHAPTER NINETEEN

verse 30 (2)

Moreover whom he did predestinate, them he also called:
and whom he called, them he also justified: and whom
he justified, them he also glorified.

2. Them he also justified

Justification follows so closely, so surely, upon our calling that it is spoken of as already done. The Lord has decreed, engaged and promised that when he begins he will make an end. All whom he calls, however guilty and miserable they may have been in times past, or may appear to themselves under their first awakenings, he will justify infallibly – yea whenever they can make out their calling they may conclude they are justified already.

The doctrine of justification is of the utmost importance to be well understood. An essential mistake in this will mislead the soul far from Christ and from hope. And even smaller mistakes which do not affect the foundation, yet tend greatly to discourage the believer, to make his hands hang down and his knees feeble. We may say that most of the fears and conflicts the children of God are exercised with about their acceptance and state are owing to their not being established in this point. It is therefore the business of ministers to make it as plain as possible; but when we have done all, it is only the Spirit of God can give an experimental knowledge of the peace and happiness of a justified state.

This being the leading truth of the gospel – for according to a man's views of justification such is his experience and such is his preaching if a minister – it has been largely treated of by many champions for the faith – some in a more learned, some in a more experimental manner. But we are so happy here as to have little occasion to meddle with controversies. I shall have occasion to speak of it again from verse 33. At present I shall endeavour to describe and illustrate it in plain words under three particulars:

1. What it is to be justified.
2. How we are justified.
3. When we are justified.

2.1 What it is to be justified

Justification is properly a *law* word and answers nearly to *acquitted* with us. Suppose an action was brought against a man in court for a great sum of money. There are two ways in which he might be acquitted:

If he could plead and prove that the demand was unjust, in this case the law which would otherwise have cast him, becomes his friend and he receives such a public honourable discharge as throws shame upon his accusers and prevents him having any farther trouble upon that account.

Or:

If the man should confess the debt and yet produce a friend that had or would pay the whole, the event would be the same – the law would be satisfied and the man discharged. The payment made by another on his behalf would answer the same purpose and free him from any farther demand, just as if he had paid the whole himself.

Now all the children of Adam are debtors to the justice of God and sooner or later his holy law will take them every one of them (as it were) by the throat and say, Pay me that which thou owest. Its demands are exceeding heavy for it will be content with no less than the uttermost farthing and in case of failure it requires the destruction of soul and body in hell. Now those who have an answer ready that will satisfy the Law and make it release its claim against them, are justified. For the very same justice which otherwise would have given sentence against them, will plead in their behalf, will forbid their going into the pit and will give them a title to all the blessings which the sentence of the law would have deprived them of. They are acquitted from all charge and penalty and admitted to all the privileges of the children of God.

But

(i) This cannot be done in the first way, by denying the debt. Those who in their own names will dare to plead not guilty must expect no mercy (Luke 19.22).

(ii) Neither can any that are in their right minds present that plea (Matt. 18.29). Those who think they can, know little of God or of themselves.

(iii) Sink then we must under the dreadful load, unless we can find a friend that will undertake for us, a friend willing and able to say to the Law, If they have wronged thee or owe thee ought, I have or will repay it – and such a welcome friend the gospel brings to our knowledge. O ye redeemed, rejoice and wonder! O ye guilty lift up your heads and hope. Jesus has paid the debt and allows every poor trembling soul to make use of his name. And when we can do this in faith, a peace and calm of mind, something like the taking a mountain from off the breast, brings a proof that by him we are justified from all things. This leads:

2.2 How are we justified

We may consider justification twofold, as it respects God and
our own consciences.

(i) In the first sense, we are justified solely and entirely by
the righteousness of Christ, that is his obedience to the commands of the law and his suffering the penalties due to sin,
considered and taken together as one great complete undertaking on our behalf. The just and holy God does not,
will not (I would speak it with reverence), cannot, forgive
one sin upon any other account (Matt. 3.17; Gal. 3.13; Rev.
5.9).

(ii) As justification respects our consciences and state, it is
by faith. The moment we believe we are justified. There is
a treasure fund in the righteousness of Christ sufficient to
clear and deliver every debtor, and each particular person
acquires a right to it by believing. God is in Christ reconciling the world to himself. The way is always open, the
reconciliation actually effected by faith uniting the sinner
to the Saviour (Rom. 5.1). His readiness and sufficiency to
save was set forth by the cities of refuge under the Law.

2.3 *When* are they thus justified?

There are two very wide opinions upon this point:

(i) Some will not allow a person to be justified till they
have either some sudden impression or manifestation upon
their minds. But as these are hard to be described, easy to
be counterfeited, so there are many who never had them,
who may be proved to be in a justified state. Thus:

(a) All who have true faith in Christ are justified (Acts
13.39).

(b) No man can truly love Christ, grace and holiness, renounce all confidence in the flesh etc., without true faith.

(c) Many give these evidences of faith who cannot conclude much in their own favour. Yet they have received the Spirit of Christ and therefore must be justified, for with the wicked he does not dwell.

(ii) Some go to a contrary extreme and plead for an external justification. It is true the Lord knows them that are his and his purpose towards them, but they are no more justified before they are called than they are called before they are born into the world.

(iii) The answer I would give to this question *When*, is in these particulars:

(a) It is possible the precise moment of passing from death unto life, of receiving that precious faith which gives us an interest in a whole Saviour, is known only to God and has already taken place before it can be perceived or reflected on.

(b) In some however it is very quickly and remarkably evident. Perhaps they were upon the brink of despair giving up all for loss and the Lord broke in upon them on a sudden – yet it is not certain that they had not before that true faith in the promises which enabled them to cry and plead for mercy.

(c) Justification in the sight of God is perfect at once, but the knowledge of it in the conscience is for the most part gradual, as faith and the knowledge of Christ increase. But my text proves expressly that all who are effectually called are certainly justified.

Therefore:

1. Are you called? Have you scriptural evidence of a change of heart? You may safely conclude a change of state. So the Apostle teaches us to reason in one effect of grace (1 John 3.14). So we may reason with regard to any other.

2. If you are not called, you are not justified, you are still in your sins. And can you go home in peace knowing this? If not justified, the law, the justice, the power of God, is against you and how soon you may be laid hold of who can tell? O flee for refuge to the hope set before you.

CHAPTER TWENTY

verse 30 (3)

*Moreover whom he did predestinate, them he also called:
and whom he called, them he also justified: and
whom he justified, them he also glorified.*

3. Them he also glorified
The close of the verse gives us the last and highest link of the
golden chain of salvation. The work of the Lord is perfect, he
does nothing by halves – he does not call sinners by his Spirit
and justify them freely by his grace and then leave them to
shift for themselves. If it was so, none could be saved – for the
evil heart of unbelief would lead us back into sin and misery if
he was not engaged by his covenant love to secure his people
to the end. This is the point that chiefly lies in the word. Of
that state of glory to which his people shall be brought we
have had occasion to speak once or twice in the course of the
lecture, particularly from verse 18. The point which now opens
to us and which is more largely insisted on in the following
verses is the final perseverance of the saints. But there is one
thing to be cleared by the way. It seems at first sight as if there
was a link wanting in this chain, for here is no mention of
sanctification – though it is expressly said in one place and
confirmed by the strain of the whole scripture that without
holiness no man shall see the Lord. I answer, though it is not
expressly mentioned, it is clearly implied in each of the other
words in the verse. If we compare scripture with scripture:

1. In the predestination
As we showed from the last verse – the end asserted is to be
conformed to the image of his son. So Ephesians 1.4.

2. In the calling

We observed it is a holy calling, from the bondage of sin and Satan to the free and honourable service of God.

3. In the justification

God justifies the ungodly and thereby delivers them from ungodliness. They no longer continue what they were. That gracious faith which unites them to Jesus purifies their hearts, worketh by love and overcomes the world.

4. In the glorification

Grace is glory begun. They are renewed into the glorious image of their Saviour and this is holiness. It is indeed but imperfect and faint in comparison of their future honour, so that it does not yet appear what they shall be, but in comparison of what they were and had by nature, it is exceeding glorious. There is a glory in the first degrees of grace (Prov. 12.26). And as they are enabled to see more of the glory of Christ in the glass of the gospel they are changed into the same image from glory to glory (2 Cor. 3.18). They have already received the first fruits, the same in kind, though of an inferior degree, with that glory which shall be revealed in them. And this is a pledge of the whole payment.

That those who have received grace and faith, who are called and justified, shall surely attain to heavenly glory, is a truth full of comfort and very necessary to uphold our fainting spirits. We shall have occasion to notice the objections which unbelief would raise against it, as we go through the remaining part of the chapter. At present I shall confine myself to the direct proof of it and this lies in such reasons as these:

3.1 The unchangeableness of God

If he had been pleased to let us perish there needed nothing more than to leave us to ourselves. But since he loved us with an everlasting love, loved us when we were enemies, loved us so as to give his Son, his only Son, for our sakes, sent his gospel by his providence to our ears and by his Spirit gave it entrance in our hearts, we may humbly hope that he will not now cast us off – this comfort might arise from the single knowledge of his unchangeableness. But we have besides:

3.2 His express promises
(Jer. 31.40; Isa. 54.9,10.) And that these are free and sure, not to be overturned by our unworthiness, is particularly confirmed in Psalm 89.30-34.

3.3 The union with Christ affected by faith, so intimate that believers are said to be members of his body, his flesh and his bones. Those whom God has thus joined together can by no means be put asunder. By this union they are interested in:

(i) His death
It is ever available on their behalf. Hence it is said to be [προσφατον][17] (Heb 10.20). The word properly signifies newly slain. His blood is still fresh and efficacious as when first shed (Heb. 7).

(ii) His life
This is secure. Having once died he dieth no more – and he has said, Because I live, *ye shall live also* (John 14.19).

(iii) His inheritance
In verse 17 of this chapter. If we are joint heirs with him and as the Son abideth in the house forever (John 8.35), the consequence is plain and comfortable.

(iv) His victories
He fought and conquered for us. And though he suffers his

vanquished enemies to show their head against his people, he will not permit them to rob him.

(v) His intercession
We may ground the whole upon this point. Since we have his own word that he does pray and for what (Luke 22.32; John 17). And the extent of this intercession we learn from Hebrews 7.25.

3.4 The beginnings of the spiritual life are in their own nature connected with everlasting life (John 6.54 and 4.14). Upon this ground alone such promises as Matthew 5.6 are sure of accomplishment. If the perseverance is not secured, it might be that a person should truly hunger and thirst after righteousness and yet never be filled. So should the word of God be of none effect.

Upon such strong arguments as these the Apostle gives that challenge with which the chapter concludes. He was well acquainted with the Christian warfare, how fiercely the soul that loves Jesus is sure to be assaulted – he was well acquainted with the heart of man, how weak, deceitful and prone to wander. Yet says he with a holy triumph, *Who* shall separate us from the love of Christ? And every believer stands upon the same foundation and has equal right to say the same things. While Jesus is the foundation, root, head and husband of his people, while the word of God is yea and amen, while the counsels of God are unchangeable, while we have a Mediator and High Priest appointed of God, while the Holy Spirit is willing and able to bear witness to the truth of the gospel, while God is wiser than men and stronger than the devil, so long the believer in Jesus is, and shall be, safe.

By way of improvement of this comfortable truth I shall close with two or three advices to suit different persons amongst us.

1. Do not mistake it

The question does not concern the hearers or professors of the gospel any farther than as believers. Some who contend for this truth seem to suppose that all who plead for it must be interested in it. But another question depends upon this. The Lord takes care of them that are his, but are you one of them? His foundation stands sure, but are you built upon it? Here you may see the necessity of prayer, watchfulness and obedience, that you may make your calling and election sure and may know that not only the doctrine is true to others, but that it is yours, that the thing is true both in him and in you, as the Apostle speaks in another case.

2. Do not abuse it

Remember there is that in believers themselves that may tempt them to abuse the doctrines of grace. And they do when they are either slack in the use of means or when they venture upon forbidden things. If you are a child you will not be lost at the end. But carelessness and disobedience may fill your heart with bitterness and make you cry out of broken bones by the way.

3. Do not forget it

But if you have fled to Jesus for refuge, feed upon the comfort here set before you: plead it in your prayers, press it upon Satan in his temptations and rejoice in it under all your troubles. The kingdom is reserved for you in heaven and you shall be kept for it upon earth till your warfare is finished and then you shall be brought home with shouts of triumph and songs of everlasting praises.

CHAPTER TWENTY-ONE

verse 31

What shall we then say to these things? If God be for us,
who can be against us?

The Apostle having enumerated all the privileges, honours
and comforts of a believer from his first deliverance from condemnation to his certain entrance into glory – unable to go
any higher – now makes a stand and breaks out into a lively
expression of admiration and praise. We may call this the conclusion, winding up and sum of the whole discourse. The triumph first in general terms in this and the next verse – the
Christian need *fear* nothing for God is on his side; can *want*
nothing, for in the great gift of his Son, God has given him all.
He afterwards triumphs particularly first over sin – who shall
accuse? – who condemn? – verses 33, 34. Secondly over affliction and trouble – who shall separate? And having mentioned the chief things which are terrible to our senses and
challenged all the powers of the invisible world, he concludes
that neither the one or the other shall be able to separate from
the love of God which is in Christ Jesus our Lord.

The present verse shows us the language of lively faith as
expressed in strong affection and in strong confidence.

1. A *strong* affection

There is a strong affection manifested in this short lively question, What shall we say? We may often observe the Apostle's
heart taking fire from his own words and before he is aware
he seems carried out of himself in wonder and praise. Alas
that we are so little like him! How cold and unfeeling are we
when speaking or hearing of gospel truth! O for a coal from

the altar – to enflame our hearts and lips! What *shall* we, what *ought* we, to say to these things? Considering:

1.1 The things themselves
– to be freed from condemnation – to receive the adoption – to have the first fruits in possession and glory secured by promise – to be chosen, called, justified and glorious – how many and how valuable are these things. What shall we say!

1.2 The means of conveyance ·
– the death of Jesus, as in the next verse – *God spared not his own Son*, but delivered him up for us. Herein was love. What shall we say to this!

1.3 The objects of this wonderful love
– we who were sinners and rebels. This thought affected our Apostle much (ch. 5.10).

All three are summed up together (1 John 3.1). Now what shall we say, what is actually said where these things are revealed by the gospel?

1. Too many say, in their hearts and lives at least, if not with their lips, We care not about them. We will not have this man to rule over us. We neither fear the condemnation nor desire the glory. We will do according to our own will (Jer. 44.16, 17). Is this indeed the determination of any here? Alas, what will you do hereafter, to whom will you flee for help, or where will you have your glory?

2. Some (I hope none here) say, Let us continue in sin that grace may abound. They do not so much reject the gospel as take encouragement from it to go on in their evil ways. This is, if possible, worse. O beware of abusing these things. It

would be better never to have heard of them than to turn them
to poison. But –

3. Believers will admire and praise and mix their praises with
lamentations that they can praise no more.

2. A *strong* confidence

If God be for us, who can be against us? It does not mean that
none will be against those who have the Lord on their side,
but that all opposition will be in vain.

2.1 Those who are on the Lord's side will surely have many against them (John 15.19).

Till we declare for him the world will be at peace with us,
but no longer. Satan will not trouble us while he bears a rule;
he is indeed an enemy even to natural men and seeks their
destruction both soul and body, but in a different way, by push-
ing them on to sin. But when the Lord frees them out of his
hand, he will pursue them with open malice and set all his
servants against them. While Saul was a persecutor the world
smiled and he was in a way of preferment, but when he sub-
mitted to Jesus his former friends sought his life. From that
day forwards bonds and afflictions awaited him. Therefore
we must not judge of the Lord's presence by outward dispensations, for in this respect to an eye of sense either all things
happen alike to all, or the children of God meet the largest
share of affliction. While the rich worldling is clothed in purple, believing Lazarus lodges on a dunghill, and has neither
health or food. The children of God may be known two ways:

(i) Satan fights furiously against them. He rages like Neb-
uchadnezzar.

(ii) They also fight against him. The former without this

latter is nothing worth. An outward profession may engage opposition and people may take a pleasure in it if it comes not too close. It may feed their pride and make them think themselves something. But is your heart set against his kingdom interest and will, have you renounced his service, are you made willing and desirous to forsake every evil way? If so, fear not. God is for you. None can harm you.

2.2 The difficulty is to maintain faith in exercise and to believe that God is with us when all things else seem against us.

Consider the case of Job and you may see how sorely a child of God may be pressed on every side. And scripture examples may teach us that God's presence is many different ways with his people and we find it so in our experience.

(i) By preventing the danger – they see it but it does not hurt them at all. How furious was Senacherib against Jerusalem. He was permitted to look at it at a distance, but that was all. When he thought to destroy all before him, the hook and bridle in his jaws pulled him back and sent him away disappointed. All his preparations and threatenings came to nothing.

(ii) He sometimes lets their enemies go a step farther and seemingly prevail. His people are brought into trouble but the Lord is with them there, supports them under it and brings them out without loss. So Daniel suffered no more in the den of lions than he would have done from a flock of sheep. I will be with thee etc..

(iii) Sometimes he suffers them to end their lives in trouble, but he comforts them with his presence and takes them to himself. And what harm is there in this? What did Stephen suffer though he was stoned, when he had full in view Jesus in his glory, standing to receive him! So likewise in the case of Elijah and Paul. When Elijah was to be killed at one time he could not be found. Afterwards when it was known where he was, he was still safe, for fire from heaven devoured his adversaries. And when he put himself as it were in Ahab's hands, those hands were secretly tied by the power of God, that he could not be touched. So Paul was delivered when brought before Nero the first time and he would have been delivered the second, only then his service was finished and the hour come when he must rest from his labours and enter into his master's joy.

In short, whatever our enemies are permitted to do, there are three things which they cannot do and therefore we need not fear them. They may make us weary of the world, they may drive us to prayer, they may be used as means to make us more watchful and dependent. But they cannot take from us:

1. The love which God bears us.
2. The grace which he has given us.
3. Nor the glory which he has designed us for.

To poor sinners, I may turn the words and say, If God be against you, who can be for you? What will riches profit for you in the day of wrath? What help will your vain companions who encourage you in sin do for you at last? (Isa. 28,15-18).

CHAPTER TWENTY-TWO

verse 32 (1)

He that spared not his own Son, but delivered him up for us all, how shall he not with him also freely give us all things?

Wants and fears are two considerable articles of the patrimony entailed on us by the fall of our first parents – they are inseparable from a fallen state and no condition or person is exempt from them. Fear can find a way to the heart of a king in the midst of his guards, and those who have the largest possessions are often harassed with the most numerous wants. Even the believer is greatly exposed to both, but not as a believer, for the Lord has provided enough to silence every fear and to prevent every uneasy distressing want, if we had but strong faith always in exercise to plead and live upon his word. The consideration that God is for us would then be a sufficient answer to every fear that could arise (Pss. 27.1 and 46.1,2). Nor should we be ever apprehensive of wanting anything truly good for us if we could fully enter into the meaning of this verse. We should then see and say with the Apostle *He that* – etc.. In the words we have:

1. An account of what God has done. He *spared not – delivered–*

2. An inference from hence. What he will do – *freely give all things* with him.

3. The certainty of this conclusion. He that did the one – how shall he not do the other?

1. What God had done

What God had done is taken for granted as a thing well known and surely believed. He that *spared not his own Son but delivered him up for us all*. Every word here is rich in meaning and calls for our notice and our praise, for this is the theme which shall employ the harps and songs of heaven to eternity.

1.1 The character of Christ – *God's own Son*.

The expression is emphatic. ιδιου[18] his proper own, only Son. The Lord Christ is the Son of God in a peculiar and exclusive sense:

(i) With regard to his divine nature. It is of this the Apostle speaks (Phil. 2.6). He whom John chapter 1 calls The Word, who was with God and was God.

(ii) With regard to his human nature (Luke 1.35). He was formed as a man in the virgin's womb by the immediate power of the most high. But especially:

(iii) As God and man united in one person, the Mediator, most of the texts in which Christ is called the *Son* of God (if not all) seem to have[19] a peculiar reference to his visible appearance as God manifest in the flesh. The man Jesus united to the Divine Word was the Son, the beloved Son. How loved, how lovely, our faint thought cannot conceive.

There are three especial circumstances of his life in which we may consider a little with what complacence and delight the Father rested in him.

(a) At his baptism, when he publicly entered upon his great undertaking (Matt. 3.17). And lo! a voice etc.

(b) At his transfiguration (Mark 9.3), so we call it, though improperly. His state of humiliation might rather be called his transfiguration, for on the mount he shone forth in his own glory.

(c) Before his passion, when he commended his people to God in his prayer and professed his complete universal obedience to the divine will (John 17.4).

Thus high, thus honoured, thus beloved, was he of whom it is said:

1.2. He spared him not.
This may be understood two ways:

(i) He would not withhold him, when our salvation could be no otherwise affected. *This* circumstance should affect us with a sense of the excellency of:

(a) The love of God
His goodness [descends in the sun and is][19] brought to our ears by every blast of wind. He feeds and clothes all his creatures. But his love, his matchless love, can only be known from this his best gift. Herein he has commended his love (Rom. 5.8, [συνιστησι])[20] placed in the fairest light, the most striking view, to captivate and subdue our stubborn hearts.

(b) Of Christ
None but Jesus. This was in effect the language of the law and well may be ours. No inferior satisfaction could be accepted. To suppose otherwise would be to reproach the wisdom of God in giving his beloved Son to so much suffering without absolute ne-

cessity (Gal. 3.21 and 2.21). Christ is the only foundation. Wo to those who reject him. Such will be
founded foolish builders when the day of trial comes.
Beware that you put nothing in the stead and place
of Christ, lest you and your hopes sink into everlasting ruin and you see and bewail your error when it is
too late.

(c) Of the soul
See what a price the Lord has given to redeem it and
will you make light of it? Consider your soul is im-
mortal. It will live when your body is in the dust. It
will live to meet your body again. Again, consider
this never dying soul has a never ceasing capacity
for happiness and misery. O what a *blessing* to be a
man, if we are renewed by grace. A little while you
must endure the trials of mortality, but ere long you
shall be as the angels, you shall mount up as with
eagles' wings to the courts of the Most High and then
you shall be forever with the Lord. O what a *curse* to
be a man – to die without an interest in Christ. Better
far to have been a beast – a dog, a toad, or a serpent.
You may have a little longer space to walk in a vain
show, but if death finds you out of Christ, you must
then be partaker with devils – the wrath of God, the
stings of conscience, the malice of Satan, will fill
you with weeping and wailing and gnashing of teeth
for ever. These things give the soul such an importance in the eyes of him who made it, that he spared
not his own Son. But the word *spared not* has another sense and implies:

(ii) He would not abate him any thing when he had undertaken to stand in the place of sinners. Having engaged to

pay our debt, the very utmost farthing was exacted. Though
he was the Father's own Son. Therefore:

(iii) Let sinners tremble before the justice of God.
If Jesus suffered, shall you escape? Surely he that spared
not his own Son will not spare *you*, if you are found at last
under the curse of the law.

(iv) Let poor convinced souls lift up their hopes.
Take comfort. Are you afraid of punishment for sin, though
you are desirous to flee to Jesus for safety? Why, there is
no punishment left for you, Jesus has borne it all. The cup
is quite empty, Jesus did not give up the ghost till he drank
the last drop and could say it was finished. He was not
spared, therefore you shall not be touched. Only believe.
Chastisements and tribulations you may meet with but there
is now no condemnation to them that are in him. For he
was not spared. Yea:

1.3 He delivered him up (Acts 2.23)

The word there properly is a military term when a person,
upon some agreement, or for some offence, is delivered up
into the hands of the enemy to be treated as they please. Thus
the Lord Jesus according to the counsel and decree of God
was given up for sins not his own into the hands of cruel,
bloodthirsty foes. The enemy of God and man, by himself,
and by his instruments, inflicted the utmost upon the head of
the innocent hostage who had undertaken to rescue multitudes
of poor sinners out of his hands. In this he and his instruments
were executioners of the curse of the law and there were sufferings beyond their power to inflict; it pleased the Father to
bruise him, and to make his soul an offering for sin. This would
be a fit occasion to speak of what he endured when he bore
away the curse from us – but that our time will not permit it.
There remains:

1.4 The expression: *For us all*

The word *all* here is to be limited and explained by the context. All who were foreknown. All who shall be called and justified in time and admitted to glory in the day of the Lord. All who are so united to Christ by faith that nothing shall separate them from him, but they shall be surely made more than conquerors. These have nothing to fear, for God is on their side; they shall never want, for God in giving his own Son for them has given them a sure right in every good – of this we must speak hereafter.

Do we indeed believe these things? Such I address in our Lord's words – Blessed are your eyes for they see – your ears for they hear. Pray for larger measures of faith, that you may live more happily, more above the world, more to the praise of his glorious grace, more to the commendation of your profession in the sight of men. It becomes those where much has been forgiven and much received, to love much, to obey, to trust and to rejoice in hope of the glory that shall be revealed.

CHAPTER TWENTY-THREE

verse 32 (2)

He that spared not his own Son, but delivered him up for us all, how shall he not with him also freely give us all things?

The knowledge of Christ, like the sun, diffuses light upon every object. It discovers a glorious prospect through and beyond the dark valley of death and shows a refuge and provision in all the troubles and difficulties of life. If God has not spared his own Son, we may well trust him for everything else. This inference the Apostle here makes for us and teaches us to conclude upon this ground:

2. What he will do

That with him he will freely give us all things. May the Lord enable you that are acquainted with your wants to feed sweetly upon this promise.

2.1 All blessings and gifts are in effect contained in the gift of Christ

Consider man in his lost estate, as a sinner, and he had forfeited all – not only spiritual but temporal. He not only lost a right to glory, but to the commonest mercies of life – bread, water and air – and had there not been a remedy provided, the earth would have doubtless refused to yield food to those who were in rebellion against their Maker. The sentence of death must have instantly taken place. But the great God having intended to enrich those with blessings whom sin had made miserable and poor, he gave his Son first by promise and in the fullness of time in our nature to remove the hindrances which otherwise must have withheld his bounty from us. His justice being now satisfied, his injured honour repaired, God can now in a way worthy of himself communicate his goodness to sinners. And the communications of his goodness are extensive, free and fully suited to the nature and necessities of his creature where sin is not the bar – his goodness has a full effect, like the light of the sun which, when the interposing wall or cloud is removed, shines forth upon the eye with its whole power and fills it to its utmost capacity of receiving (James 1.5, 17). Thus all in effect is given in Christ because he has removed all the reasons why anything was withheld.

2.2 All things are actually committed to the Son for the use of his people (Col. 1.19; John 3.35)

Jesus by his death procured us a right to every blessing and he now lives to disperse and bestow them in such measures and seasons as he sees most suitable for our good. If we could believe this, that all our dispensations are directed by him, who bowed his head for us upon the accursed tree (cross), how safely might we trust him, how comfortable might we live casting our care upon him, when we have such a strong argument to convince us that he careth for us?

2.3 The faith of the operation of God which unites the soul to Christ gives us (that is all who believe) an express right, propriety and entrance, to all that Jesus has received for his people

No man by law, custom or profession, has so good and sure a title to any thing he can call his own as the believer has to everything he wants from God. *All* is yours if you are Christ's.

Consider:

(i) The general tenor of the covenant of grace – the design was that those who are poor should be made rich.

(ii) The many express and particular promises such as Psalm 84.11, Philippians 4.19. Will the Lord break his word and alter the thing that has gone out of his lips? Good reason therefore there is for this conclusion – and for the strong manner of the expression, which is the point I was to speak to:

3. *How much more? q.d.* How can you doubt it!

Do you not plainly see, it is impossible it should be otherwise? Arguments may be drawn.

3.1 From the greater to the less

What comparison is there between delivering up his Son, and any other gifts? Christ was an expensive gift indeed. God had nothing like him to bestow. But since he spared not his own Son, every other gift is cheap and easy.

3.2 From the difference of states

God gave his Son to die for the ungodly, when *we were yet sinners*. How then shall he refuse smaller things to those whom he has called by his grace and taught to fear him?

3.3 God was no ways bound to provide a Saviour

He might justly have left us to perish. But in and through the Son of his love he has now been pleased to bind himself by promises and oaths that he will freely give everything else.

Here then is strong consolation to those who are called by grace. What is your fear? It is a vain fear. What is your want? It shall surely be supplied, God is yours, Christ is yours, life and death, things present and things to come – all are yours.

Only to answer the unbelieving cavils which are now perhaps at work in your hearts, I would have you notice a few things:

1. The Lord has not *so* given you all things that you shall be your own carers and have everything in your possession that your vain hearts may desire. And well it is for you that he has not, for you would soon ruin yourselves. Have not you found that when he has indulged you a good deal in this way, you were growing worldly, careless and secure apace – and if he had not in mercy checked you by denials and crosses, or by breaking the reed you was leaning on, you know not where you had been? Therefore:

2. He will not *so* give you all things, as that you shall not have daily occasion to feel the vanity and insufficiency of the creature and the necessity of continual dependence upon himself. If you are believers you must live a life of faith. You must be content to pray and believe and wait for your mercies before you have them. You must go without some things which you think you want, that you may learn that the Lord is wiser than you.

3. For those things which the Lord does intend to give you, he has an appointed time and for this you must wait on him. Here the impatience and depravity of our hearts often discovers itself. If the Lord does not answer us the next minute, we complain that he takes no notice (Isa. 49.14).

4. The Lord takes care both of soul and body, yet so as that his great design is to the better part. A house is repaired not for the building's sake, but on account of those who dwell in it. His purpose is to promote your sanctification, therefore he may and often will keep you short of small blessings, that you

may be fitted for greater. This consideration cuts off all your objection – about sickness, poverty, loss of friends etc. – for these afflictions and trials are among the all things which the Lord has promised freely and surely to give to his people. They are instruments for good. Each in their place have a part in helping you forward in the divine life exercising your graces and ripening you for glory.

5. You must therefore understand this promise with these limitations:

    5.1 All that he sees necessary.

    5.2 Each, *when* he sees best.

Go then with this promise to the throne of grace – pray first to know your own state and wants and to have your desires moulded by his word and will, and then be careful about nothing but in everything by prayer and supplication make your request known unto God. And you shall not pray in vain. He that spared not his own Son will freely give you everything else – *grace*, peace, wisdom, provision and protection.

But we must not conclude without taking notice that this promise is confined to believers – to those I mean who are seeking the Lord for their salvation and portion. To others, if you reject God's best and greatest gift, what right have you to expect any other good from him? Nay, even the things which by his permission you do enjoy you have no right to – nor have you his blessing in the use of them. Blessings they are in themselves, but not to *you* if you are out of Christ and contentedly so. Hear that awful threatening (Mal. 2.2). Alas there is a curse upon every house and upon every heart where the fear of God does not dwell. Your gold and silver in which you place your confidence – your health and strength – your relations and employments – a secret eating curse is mixed with them all.

The curse of a broken law is upon you and the more your
hearts are blinded with a show of pleasure here, so much the
heavier will be your misery if you should die under this curse.
Then you must give a strict account of all you have abused.
And what will you answer? As yet there is hope. The Lord
has bent his bow and pointed his arrow at you. You stand as
the mark of his justice, yet still he is long suffering. Shall not
this goodness lead you to repentance? Will you not humble
yourselves – you have been often warned, remember Prov-
erbs 29.1. Awake and look to Jesus. He and he only can deliver you. He was given for sinners – he was not spared – he
suffered – he rose – he is able to save to the uttermost.

CHAPTER TWENTY-FOUR

verse 33

Who shall lay any thing to the charge of God's elect?
It is God that justifieth.

From the general triumph of faith in the two preceding verses the Apostle now descends to enumerate and examine the particular things which might withstand the believer's peace. The first of these and the chief cause of every other evil is sin. It might be said – True they are well secured when God is for, and well provided for to whom he has given all things freely with his Son, but while faith is weak the power of guilt and corruption keeps the soul low. But O that you could believe this word – *Who shall lay?* Not that they are strictly speaking unblameable, on the contrary they have fallen short in all things and there are many ready to plead their defects against them. But if a charge is cut groundless it would be in vain. For they have surety who has undertaken their cause and discharged all their debts. Christ has not only died for them but rose again and is so far from being weary or sorry for all that he has done, that he now continually makes intercession for them, so that the voice which prevails against them must be more powerful than his. Still more (if more can be) the Judge is on their side and has promised to justify them, to acquit them honourably before assembled worlds; neither will this be an act of mere mercy but the highest illustration of his perfect inflexible righteousness (compare Rom. 3.26). Who then shall lay anything to the charge of God's elect?

Every clause, every word in this challenge of faith is full of meaning and would open a wide field to our meditations, notwithstanding we have had occasion to speak of the same subjects from the former verses. But I shall endeavour to avoid unnecessary repetitions and consider them as they come in my way this second time in something of a different light. We may in this verse take notice of:

1. the persons: *God's elect.*
2. their safety or indemnity: *Who shall lay...?*
3. the reason: *It is God himself that justifieth.*

1. God's elect

So 1 Peter 1.2; Titus 1.1. As the Apostle before laid the ground of our hope in God's predestination, so he now gives God all the honour. The people of God are in themselves different as to their tempers and conduct from others, but the Apostle does not lay the stress of his argument on this and say they are safe because better than others, but chiefly because he has chosen them. He proposes to us the same ground of comfort which he lived upon himself, where he is giving an account to his beloved Timothy of the views with which he looked forward to the great day. Though he had been singularly forward in his call and experience and honoured with much usefulness, he says not a word of this, but rests all upon his knowledge of the power, grace and faithfulness of Christ (2 Tim. 1.12). This is the same person who was so distressed with the views of his own heart in chapter 7. But when he ceased poreing upon himself and fixed his eyes upon the purpose of God in Christ, hear how he triumphs. This may teach you:

1.1 That if you would be established in comfort and peace you must go out of yourselves for it. To compare yourself with the word of God is right and necessary in its proper place, but unless you view by faith what God has done for you as well do enquire what he has done in you, your comfort and assurance will be always variable and unsteady, like your changing frames. You will be still up and down.

1.2 That though the Lord acknowledges and accepts his own work in his people, yet his reserving them finally to himself is in consequence of his own purpose and for the sake of his covenant in Christ. Their graces are so mixed with defilement, they come so far short in every good thing, that if he was strict to mark what is amiss they could not stand before him. But when he beholds them as chosen and accepted in the beloved, he sees no spot or blemish in them and gives them boldness upon this ground to stand before him with confidence – both at the bar of conscience here and hereafter at the great tribunal. They may triumph in their complete security and say:

2. Who shall lay anything to their charge?

As I said before, this is not a protestation of innocence. They are conscious of many things amiss and they find by experience that these are laid to their charge, but the point in question here is concerning their state and final acceptance. In this respect all charges come short and are unable to reach them. The Lord has provided them an answer. They are charged:

2.1 By conscience

(i) With sin past

The sins of their times of ignorance. Though these shall not be imputed, the remembrance remains and is useful in the hand of God to promote:.

(a) thankfulness (1 Tim. 1.13-15)
(b) humility (1 Cor. 15.9; Titus 1.3)

(ii) With innumerable infirmities and defects

These are startling to young believers, but when we are instructed in the knowledge of Christ as our righteousness, though we loathe ourselves on the account of them we are not cast down.

(iii) With actual sins and backslidings

These indeed cause a breach which only the Lord can heal.

2.2 By Satan

He observes no measures with them but as the Lord restrains him.

(i) He accuses them of all that is indeed amiss. He musters up and aggravates all their evils. When he sees that they are broke off from him, from tempter he turns accuser.

(ii) He lays to their charge things that they knew not. Calls them hypocrites, deceivers, etc..

(iii) Much in the spirit of Satan are the charges believers meet with from the world.

(a) They watch them closely, to see if they can find anything unsuitable to their profession: they expect more from them than others and if they fall, how does the world rejoice, aggravate and publish. Take care, pray to the Lord to keep you, for if you fall into the hands of men they will show you no favours.

(b) They set things in the worst light possible, where they are not evil. Any little mistake or imprudence, they charge upon them as wilful etc..

(c) When occasion is not given them, they will not stick to invent and publish falsehood – throw all the dirt they can, in hopes that at least some will stick, or that if they cannot hurt them, they may grieve them. But such reproach is indeed an honour and ground of rejoicing.[22]

(iv) The hardest charge to bear is when the Lord himself is the party. Job speaks of this (chapter 13.26; so Psalm 90.8).

The Lord has times and ways of speaking to the hearts of his people and making them smart for their folly, but this is for their chastisement and correction, not to their condemnation. Though he cause grief he will have compassion (1 Cor. 11.32). Notwithstanding any or all these charges, they are and shall be preserved. Every accusation will be overruled by the pleas mentioned here – Christ has died for sin and lives to make intercession for believing sinners, therefore they need not fear, for:

3. It is God that justifieth

3.1 *Who?* God
The supreme determination is lodged with him and the matter can be carried no higher. If God speaks none can reverse it (Lam. 3.37).

3.2 *What?* Justifieth
This is:

(i) A complete act – not the pardon of one sin only but of all (1 John 1.7). And not pardon only, but acceptance and honour – they are accounted righteous.

(ii) It is a solemn act. Not wholly of mercy, though the richest mercy to us, but it is an act of justice likewise (1 John 1.9). And all who are grieved at it are here challenged (if they can or dare) to say anything against it.

(iii) It is a final unalterable act. Not justified today and afterwards condemned. Whom he once receives he never puts away. When he loves he loves to the end.

(iv) It is a silencing act. When the soul views its justification by the blood of Christ, when by the Holy Spirit it is enabled to appeal and rest there, then it has an answer to every one that opposes. It acknowledges the charge of conscience but says, *though I am poor and needy the Lord* careth for me. It can turn upon Satan and say, All this and more I have done but Jesus has died. It can be quiet under the reproach of the world and say *'Let them curse but bless them.'* Yea it can plead with the Lord himself and say, I have sinned and done very foolishly, but I see thy mercies are infinite, thy promise sure. Though a poor sinner, I must hope and believe thou art my God still.

But especially at the Great Day. It will be a public act. Then every tongue that rises in judgment shall be condemned. Then Satan shall be confounded forever. The men of the world shall be astonished and cry, *Is* not this he whose life we accounted madness? Conscience shall rejoice in the sight of Jesus eye to eye. The Judge shall ratify their justification before all the world. Complaints and fears shall cease forever and endless joy and triumph take place.

Appreciation:
1. Poor sinners what will you do in the great day if Satan should stand forth to accuse and demand his prey and Jesus is not your friend to rebuke him?

2. Awakened souls give all diligence to make your calling and election sure. If you read, pray and walk in obedience, your faith will surely strengthen.

3. You that hope you are already justified, stir up your hearts to feed upon your privilege. God is yours, Christ is yours, all is yours. What then will you render? Your bounden duty is your highest honour. Walk humbly with your God. Abstain from every evil. Rejoice in hope.

CHAPTER TWENTY-FIVE

verse 34 (1)

*Who is he that condemneth? It is Christ that died, yea
rather, that is risen again, who is even at the right hand of
God, who also maketh intercession for us.*

That there are many ready enough to accuse we have seen
from the former verse. But who, says the Apostle, will dare to
condemn the people of God? Though there is much amiss in
them, witnessed by conscience, heavily charged by Satan,
much which they have cause to blush and be ashamed of before the Lord – yet there is no condemnation to them that are
in Christ Jesus – here is plea upon plea, sufficient to silence
every accusation from without, and every fear that riseth from
within. If any would impeach the hope of the true believer to
effect, they must prove that Christ did not die, or that he did
not rise, or that he was not admitted into the kingdom on our
behalf, or that he has forgot his promise to make intercession
for us. But while these points remain sure, the cause of every
soul that has fled to Jesus cannot miscarry.

The several particulars in this verse are so important, so
full of food and consolation that I hope it will not seem tedi-
ous if I employ one discourse upon each. It will not be so, I
am sure if the Lord the Spirit is pleased to favour us with his
presence and blessing. For this may we unite our hearts in
prayer. It is his office to take of the things of Jesus and show
them to his people.

1. It is Christ that died
The first point that offers is the death of Christ, and the ground
his death affords, for each of his people to lift up their heads
and say, Who shall condemn? Christ has died.

Consider:
1. Who? Christ.
2. What? He died.

1.1 Christ

The word *Christ* includes the person and the office of our dear Redeemer, and will lead us to consider the cause and nature of his undertaking.

(i) When we speak of Christ as a person, we mean *him* who being in the beginning, God with God, humbled himself into the form of a servant, assumed a body by the power of the Holy Ghost of the virgin Mary, and thus taking our nature upon him, became God, manifest in the flesh, full of grace and truth to those who beheld his glory, though the glory was hid from common eyes, under the veil of a suffering state. This mysterious union of God and man in one person, is incomprehensible to the perverted reason of fallen man (1 Cor. 12.3). But it is the solid rock on which the faith and hope of the church and each believer is built (Matt. 16.18). Here are two things that are necessary and sufficient to engage our confidence:

(a) His own almighty power.

(b) His nearness and relation to us (Eph. 5.30).

(ii) If we consider the name *Christ* as a peculiar epithet of the Redeemer (it signifies *One Anointed* as the Hebrew word Messiah likewise does), it presents to our faith the consideration of his appointment, his offices and the fullness of grace with which he is anointed by the Spirit, as Mediator, for the discharge of them.

(a) *His appointment*

He was properly authorised, set apart and appointed of God to be Saviour of sinners, and that in a twofold respect:

(1) *Before time*

We have express declaration of a covenant of grace established in Christ before the foundation of the world, according to the tenor of which all following dispensations took place (Prov. 8.23-31, Ps. 40.6,7 compared with Heb. 10.5). Isaiah 53.11 and many other passages in the Old Testament refer to this transaction. The Son engaged for man to God and for God to man. And on this ground he was the immediate Ruler and Lord of the church from the beginning (Acts 7.38).

(2) *In time*

We read that the Spirit descended on him and a voice pointed him out as the beloved, in and for whose sake God was well pleased. Then perhaps it was that that passage was eminently fulfilled: Isaiah 61.1. This reminds one of:

(b) *His offices*

Under the law we read that persons were solemnly anointed with holy oil for several offices, in which they were to be types of this great Anointed who was [to] unite their several offices into himself. The holy oil was poured upon:

(1) Prophets, as Elisha (1 Kings 19.16)
(2) Priests, as Aaron (Lev. 8.12)
(3) Kings, as David (1 Sam. 16.12)

Thus our Lord Jesus the Prophet, Priest and King of his church, bears the name of *the Christ* to remind us that he is authorised of God to act in all these relations and that he has voluntarily and freely accepted them for us (Pss. 2.2; 45.7; Acts 4.27; 10.38).

(c) It farther signifies the fullness of all graces residing in him. There are many anointed, but he alone bears the name of Christ *the anointed*, by way of eminence. For God gave him not the Spirit by measure. It pleased the Father that in him should all fullness dwell and that of his fullness his people might receive and grace for grace.

This is the divine the glorious person of whom it is said:

1.2 He died

A short description of his sufferings. No particulars are mentioned of the cross, nails, thorns and spear. He died includes them all. But it becomes us to consider:

(i) How he died

What more mournfully pleasing than to walk to Gethsemane and Golgotha with our suffering Lord, to read the history of his passion till we almost think we see him prostrate on the cold ground, pouring forth his soul in prayers and tears, in tears of blood, when that dreadful agony came upon him. Then to follow him in our thoughts as he was torn away by the rude multitude – buffeted and spit on in the high priest's hall, mocked by Herod and the soldiers, scourged with whips, crowned with thorns, pierced with spikes, and lifted high upon the cross. Yet let us not be so taken up with his outward sufferings as to forget that more dreadful anguish of soul which made him cry out, My God. Such was the death of the beloved Son of God in whom was all his delight. We are therefore farther to ask:

(ii) Why he died

Much might be said but time grows short and I hope this in one or other view is our constant theme.

(a) He died for sin
  (1) To show what sin was.
  (2) To remove it (John 1.29).
Sin could not be past by without atonement, therefore when it was found upon Jesus, by imputation, it cost him his life.

(b) He died for sinners that they might live. Matchless love! He needed not have died if he would have consented that we should perish.

(c) He died to take away the sting of death from his people. What is said of the bee is true here, the sting of death stuck fast in Jesus and was left in his grave. Since that, death has been harmless (though often affrightens) to believing souls.

(d) He died to put this triumphant challenge in our mouths and to say, Who shall *condemn*? By his death the law is magnified, justice satisfied and Satan conquered (Col. 2.15).

What then have awakened souls to do, but to pray for faith in this precious Saviour that they may account his life, his death, his righteousness, his victories their own! A sight of the death of Christ will make you die likewise to the world, sin and self.

But comfortless they indeed to whom this meditation affords no pleasure. If the death of Christ brings you no relief where can you find it? Is there any other sacrifice? He has said John 12.32: *[And I, if I be lifted up from the earth, will draw all men unto me.]* May it be so at this time.

CHAPTER TWENTY-SIX

verse 34 (2)

Who is he that condemneth? It is Christ that died, yea rather, that is risen again, who is even at the right hand of God, who also maketh intercession for us.

The first argument in this verse taken from the death of Christ, is a sufficient answer (as we have seen) to all who would condemn the true believer. But here is a fourfold cord not to be broken – he not only died but rose, ascended and intercedes for his people. Who then can condemn! We proceed in the contemplation of these glorious and cheering truths. The next is:

2. Christ is risen again

The *yea rather* is full of meaning qd. his love was not only great, as manifested in his dying, but victorious and successful love. He broke through death as a conqueror and thereby showed that nothing could withstand him in the undertaking he was engaged in on his people's behalf.

The resurrection of Christ, as a matter of fact, is the great pillar of Christianity. If he only died and never rose, his people are mistaken, helpless and hopeless – we are yet in our sins. But if when he was laid in the grave the grave could not detain, if he arose according to the account given of him, then I hope it will appear that we have good reason to say, Who shall condemn! Let us therefore consider:

    1. The proofs of his resurrection.
    2. The benefits of it to believers.

2.1 The proofs of his resurrection

It may seem unnecessary to prove the resurrection of Jesus – to many of you it is quite so and I shall be but brief in it. Yet I would not wholly omit it, not so much with a view to the cavils of wicked men and infidels, as for the sake of tempted souls. The enemy is very busy at times with some, in striving to beat them off from the belief of all the doctrines of scripture and this among the rest. And some who are so well convinced of this as to venture their souls upon it, are yet at a loss how to answer Satan in an hour of temptation.

Now let us suppose we received the news of some strange and almost incredible thing that had happened and consider what evidence we should require and apply the same way of reasoning to the point in hand. That there was a great while ago such a person as Jesus, who gathered disciples and was put to death upon the cross, is acknowledged universally – those who lived at the same time, Jews and heathens, though enemies to his name, not only confessed it but urged it as a reproach against his followers. Innumerable testimonies of this sort are extant to this very day.

The turning point between his enemies and his friends is the resurrection. This has been denied, for he appeared not openly as before his death, but only to a few among whom he showed himself alive by many infallible proofs. We are then to enquire who they were and upon what grounds we have to believe their testimony. Thus I say we should proceed in other cases.

(i) The eye witnesses were many (1 Cor. 15.5-8). Sufficient in number to establish the point, if their testimony may be depended upon. We can be certain of facts which we never saw, no other way. Many of you have no other evidence that there is such a place as London and many other things of which you have not the least doubt.

(ii) These witnesses could not be mistaken or deceived for they saw him not once only but often and some of them with peculiar circumstances, as Thomas, Paul, John.

(iii) Neither can they be supposed engaged in a design to deceive others with a relation which they did not believe themselves. For:

(a) They evidently appear to have been good well meaning men and to have had in view the glory of God and the good of mankind, as appears from their writings.

(b) They could propose no advantage to themselves if the thing was not true, for the very profession of believing it and especially the pains they took to publish it exposed them to the hatred of the world and sufferings of all kinds – even to death.

(c) The great effects which followed (Mark 16.20). With this doctrine, a few unknown illiterate persons prevailed mightily over sin and Satan and brought thousands into the belief of the same truth against all disadvantages. This reminds me farther of:

(d) The experimental proof. The whole Christian doctrine rests upon this point, stands and falls with it. Those therefore who have found the gospel the power of God in their own souls are made partakers of this resurrection and are sure that what brought them from darkness to light, from misery to peace, must be of God. The resurrection being established and proved, enquire:

2. 2 The benefits of it to believers
The advantages and benefits arising from it and from what reasons we may say, If Christ is risen, who shall condemn?

He arose:

(i) For our justification (Rom 4.25). That is, to prove and manifest it. If the surety is discharged, the debtor is free.

(ii) To be executor of his own will (John 17.24; Luke 22.29). Some persons' wills have been set aside and defeated after their death, but it cannot be so here.

(iii) As an example of our resurrection (1 Cor. 15.20, 23; Rom 6.5).

Are you partakers of the power of this resurrection?

1. If not – it is as yet the same to you, as though he had not rose. You are yet in your sins. But though you have not, you may. The Lord grant that this may be the hour when the dead shall hear his voice and live.

2. If you are, the subject affords:

2.1 Consolation

That divine life which you have begun to live by faith in the Son of God shall never fail. Jesus is risen to support, protect, feed, guide and guard you till he brings you home.

2.2 Exhortation

If ye are risen with Christ seek the things that are above ([i] Col 3.[1]). Let not your affections fix here – if Jesus died for your offences and rose for your justification, if he is your head, hope, husband, should not you live to him and upon him alone, devoting yourselves to his service and government that you may say, Not I but Christ liveth in me?

CHAPTER TWENTY-SEVEN

verse 34 (3)

Who is he that condemneth? It is Christ that died, yea rather, that is risen again, who is even at the right hand of God, who also maketh intercession for us.

We have endeavoured to view Jesus our Saviour as hanging on the cross for our sins and rising from the grave for our justification. Let us now by the eye of faith follow him to that heaven from which his love brought him down. He is no longer a man of sorrows, but the Lord of glory. He is ascended and seated at the right hand of God. This meditation is suited to comfort the hearts of his believing people and to put the Apostle's triumph in their mouths, Who shall condemn?

3. At the right hand of God

The right hand of God is a figurative expression spoken after the manner of man, for God is a spirit – infinite and everywhere. His presence fills heaven and earth. It does not therefore mean any determinate place where the human nature of Christ resides, but the high and excellent honour which as our Mediator, Head and Forerunner, he is there possessed of. The right hand among men is a token of pre-eminence. The meaning of the phrase is expressed more at large: Philippians 2.9-11.

It imports:

3.1 That glorious rest into which he is entered after his sufferings and labours in the work of redemption. And this thought is comfortable to his people – they love him for what he endured, their hearts melt and their eyes flow when they think of his passion and they have a proportionable joy in knowing

150

that all these things are finished. Christ being raised from the dead dieth no more.

3.2 His supreme honour and dignity. The glorious angels are standing ministering before the throne, but Jesus is seated upon the throne itself and in our nature is worshipped by all the heavenly host. He has received the government and exercises all power in heaven and earth. This likewise concerns his people, for his honour is theirs, as the wife is privileged in the dignity of her husband.

3.3 The stability of his government and glory. He is immovably seated – his enemies could not prevent his taking possession, nor can they disturb him now. In vain they rage and imagine vain things against him. He that sitteth in the heavens laugheth them to scorn (1 Cor. 15.25).

But let us consider what are those particular ends and concerns respecting his people which he has told us in his word he had expressly in view when he ascended into heaven and sat down at the right hand of the Majesty on high.

3.4 He ascended as their representative to claim and take possession in their names. By sin, mankind had lost all right and title to heaven, but one clause of the covenant of grace established with Christ was that by his obedience to death he should *bring many sons to glory* and become the author of eternal salvation to all who obey him (Heb. 2.10 and 5.9). Having therefore fulfilled the condition, he ascended with his own blood within the veil to appear in the presence of God *for them*. Hence he is styled[22] the *Forerunner* (Heb. 6.20).

3.5 He is gone to prepare a place for them (John 14.2). The kingdom is prepared from the foundation of the world – a particular place for each is prepared by Jesus – in the management he undertakes of each one's cause and concern, before the throne and in the world. If this is his design they may well say, Who shall condemn? For he will not be disappointed. Fear not little flock, it is the Father's good pleasure to give you the kingdom and it is the office of Jesus to bring you safe to it.

3.6 He ascended – to receive gifts for men (Ps. 68.18). Public gifts for the gathering in and building up his church (Eph. 4.11,12). And especially the great gift of his Holy Spirit to guide, teach, comfort his people through the wilderness (see John 16.7).

3.7 As seated on the right hand of God and having the government on his shoulder, **he maintains his cause and people against all opposition**, controls his enemies and disappoints their designs. It is because he lives and reigns, the gates of hell have not, cannot, prevail against his church. All the springs of grace are in him to supply those who are ready to faint and all the wheels of providence are under his rule to accomplish whatever he pleases. He has a hook and a bridle with which he can stop the powers of men and the powers of darkness, when they seem breaking in like a flood.

Add to all this the consideration of his intercession for us, which must be our next subject, and then say if there is any good reason to ask, Who shall condemn?

Far different must the view of this subject be to careless sinner. Do you not tremble to think that Jesus whom you crucify afresh, whose grace you slight and whose government you refuse, is seated at the right hand of God? He rules his people with a golden sceptre – but he has a rod of iron to break in pieces his enemies. How will you meet him in the great day of his wrath? Or how will you escape? Alas, the Christless sinner in that great day will neither be able to stand or to flee. Dreadful hour, when he shall say, These my enemies who would not that I should reign over them, bring them hither and slay them before my eyes.

If therefore you are not bent upon destroying your own souls seek him now while he may be found. As yet he waits to be gracious – he has the promises and pardons in his hands.

Convinced souls, when will you fight against your unbelieving fears? What complaint or burthen have you which this subject cannot relieve? Is it sin? Is it Satan? The Lord give you faith to apply what has been spoken against both.

Believers, look up to Jesus and may your affections towards him fix and raise you above the world. Let your thoughts feed on these things – where he is and what he is doing – and long to be with him.

CHAPTER TWENTY-EIGHT

verse 34 (4)

Who is he that condemneth? It is Christ that died, yea rather, that is risen again, who is even at the right hand of God, who also maketh intercession for us.

How many arguments of consolation are here as it were in a breath. The Apostle seems not to know when to stop. The source of them all however is Jesus. Paul knew no other, he preached no other, name – Christ was his all in all. Let us take pattern from him. His life, death, resurrection and ascension – either of these singly afford a sufficient answer to all who would condemn. Yet he will not stop here. He goes farther still, to his intercession. This is the subject of our present opportunity.

4. Who also maketh intercession for us
The word the Apostle uses here and in Hebrews 7.25 occurs likewise Acts 25.25, Romans 11.2 and in verse 26 of this chapter. These passages compared show that it is to be taken in a large sense – he pleads our cause, he manages our concerns, he answers our enemies. Who then shall condemn those for whom Jesus employs all his power and all his love? He pleads as a priest, he manages as a king.

4.1 He makes intercession has a plain reference to his great type, the high priest, who, according to the divine appointment, entered with blood within the veil (see the parallel, Heb. 9.7-12). Jesus is entered with his own blood. His presence and abiding in our nature, with the marks of his sufferings for us, is a continual virtual intercession. Curious questions I meddle

not with on this subject, in what ways his intercession is carried on, or whether he actually prays for his people. Of this the scripture says nothing. It is sufficient for us to know that he is there – and there on our behalf. This intercession is the great relief of a believing soul.

(i) Against guilt

Great is the distress of an awakened conscience. It dares not approach God. It dares not stay away. We may suppose the case of a person guilty of high treason and compelled to stand before the king, but no comparison can reach the case. But when such a one is enabled to look to Jesus as interceding, what light and comfort does it bring. Fear not poor mourner to draw nigh, for your peace is made, your pardon is sealed in the court above, your advocate is there waiting to introduce you. Lift up your heart to him and think you hear him in effect saying – Father there is another sinner that has heard my name and desires to trust in me. Father I will that he also may be delivered from going down to the pit and interested in the ransom that I have provided.

(ii) Under a sense of defects in duty

When we compare our best with the demands of the law, think of the majesty of our God and the defilements which pollute every thing we take in hand, we may well say, *To us belongeth shame* and confusion of face. But this humiliation is attended with comfort when we view Jesus as bearing the iniquities of our holy things – perfuming our prayers with the incense of his merit, washing our tears in his blood and covering all defects with the robe of his righteousness. We are heard and accepted in the beloved.

(iii) As supplying the poverty and narrowness of our prayers.

Of ourselves we know not what to ask and though we are

helped by the Spirit to form our petitions according to the will of God in general, yet as to particulars, we often mistake, often forget, are at times so cold, weary and wandering, that we can hardly bring a few broken words out of our mouths. It is well for us that God does more than we can ask or think, but that he does so is owing to the intercession of Christ. Jesus knows everything we want, pleads and provides accordingly. He is not negligent though we too often are. He prayed for Peter's safety before Peter was aware of his danger. Have you not been surprised to received mercies before you asked them? It was owing to the kind intercessor.

The other sense of this word respects the kingly office of Christ.

4.2 He manages
He is:

(i) The Fountain of their supplies. His eye is upon his people – he knows the time and occasion when they want support and what support they want and gives accordingly.

(ii) The Director of their dispensations. If a skilful gardener had the command of the weather he would not treat his plants always alike. He knows that all rain would drown them, all sun would burn them up. He would first consider the state of the plant and suit the weather accordingly. Thus does the great husbandman.

(iii) The Captain of their salvation that leads them forth in the spiritual conflict, teaches their hands to war and their fingers to fight and covers their head in the day of battle.

(iv) The Rebuker of their enemies, especially the great

enemy and accuser. See a specimen of his management in this respect (Zech. 3.1.5 [3.1-5?]).

We may close this part of our Apostle's triumph with such reflections as these:

1. *How precious is Jesus.* From the first step to the last, nothing can be done without him. If he had not died, we must. If he had not risen, we must have died for ever. If he had not ascended into heaven, we must have been thrust down to the lowest hell. If he did not plead for us, we have not a word to offer for ourselves. If he was not on our part, our enemies would be too hard for us. Let us then give him the glory due to him and cleave to him in love alone.

2. *How safe are his people.* Many rise up against them, but God is for them and all opposition is in vain. They are full of wants and fears, but Jesus is their Head, Surety, Saviour and Intercessor. Who then shall condemn?

3. *What an uncomfortable state to live within the knowledge of these truths yet know nothing of them.* To see this happiness with your eyes yet not taste of it. To see others pressing towards the prize and any of you to sit still till you are shut out. Think who shall condemn and who will be condemned at the great day. And may the Lord show you the things pertaining to your peace before they are hid from your eyes.

References

1. to restore to the truth, to put into practice
2. restricted
3. MSS y^e
4. is expressed in a particular style
5. MSS *ide*
6. reveal
7. MSS *you have*
8. denotes an indirect attack
9. Article 17 'Of Predestination and Election' in the Book of Common Prayer
10. confront with objections
11. present in argument, bring forward as reasons
12. followers
13. MSS / or 1 (part of an insertion)
14. James Hervey, 1714-1758, of Weston Favell, known for his clear teaching on the imputed righteousness of Christ. Romaine preached at Hervey's funeral a few years before these sermon notes were written and said of him, "What he said in words, concerning his interest in the Redeemer's righteousness, he proved by his actions ... he was humbled by the power of grace ... He never let an opportunity slip of speaking of the love of Christ ... His holy life was an excellent recommendation of his principles: for I never saw one who came up so near to the scripture character of a christian."
15. Isaac Watts, How sweet and awful is the place, verses 4 and 5
16. Chapter 12 page 70
17. MSS appears to be προσφατον
18. one's own
19. MSS *seem to have to*
20. an insertion in the MSS makes it read: *in the sun, descends in the and*
21. MSS συνιϛισι, where ϛ is the obsolete sixth letter of the Greek alphabet, diagamma
22. This point is well-illustrated in Newton's letter to William Wilberforce on 29 May 1789, following fierce opposition in Parliament to the abolition of the slave trade: 'I congratulate you, my dear Sir, on the undesigned honour Mr. Macramara has done you in the House of Commons (if the newspaper accounts of the debate may be depended on). If he had not spoken as he did, you would not have had the opportunity of making your reply, the wisdom and meekness and propriety of which will gladden the hearts of many who have not had the pleasure of being personally known to you.' Bodlein Library, MS Wilberforce, c. 49.

APPENDIX

Comments on the editing of
Newton's handwritten lecture notes.

The aim in editing was to present the text in a form that was easily readable. This chiefly involved clarifying meaning, punctuation, modernising spelling and expanding abbreviations. Some minor omissions (or additions) of underlining, italics, numbering, headings, and subheadings were made. Although in note form, Newton's text contains scarcely any errors.

For academic interest alterations are given below.

Abbreviations
The following were expanded:

NEWTON'S TEXT	EDITED TO
&c.	etc.
ag^t	against
c^d	could
L.J.	Lord Jesus
Sp.	Spirit
tow^{ds}	towards
v	verse
w^{ch}	which
w^d	would
w^n	when
wth or w^t or w^h	with
X^t	Christ
y^e	the, verse, is (see below)
(except in quotes from AV)	
y^m	them
y^r	your

Capitals
In general the modern use of the lower case appears in editing. There were inconsistencies of case in the original text for some words such as: almighty, Almighty.

Ambiguities
when and *where* were sometimes difficult to distinguish.

any thing and *every thing* occasionally appeared to be written as single words.

In one instance a word had been underlined and another word written above. The latter was used in editing as the former was indistinct. In two other instances both words have been included, as in *tree(cross)*.

The editing of *Spirit* and *spirit* was unclear in two instances in Chapters 6 and 7.

Where words have become archaic, the modern meaning, from the Oxford Dictionary, has been included in a footnote the first time it appears.

Newton used both Cant. and Song of Sol. for the Song of Solomon.

Omissions of words or uncertain inclusions are indicated with [].

The following were changed for the sake of clarity
Apostrophes have been inserted as in modern usage.

Newton's use of [] has been edited to () to avoid confusion with the editor's insertions.

Roman numerals used for main points in the original have been changed to Arabic numerals.

Scripture texts, from the Authorised Version, have been inserted in italics at the beginning of each chapter.

Question marks have occassionally been omitted in editing e.g. the statement *consider how he died?*

Chapter 1: *from ye 17 to ye close of the 25* edited to *from verse 17 to the close of verse 25.*

In Chapter 23 *the reed you was leaning on* was left as is.